WORLDS IN HARMONY

WORLDS IN HARMONY

Dialogues on Compassionate Action

His Holiness the Dalai Lama

with
Daniel Goleman
Stephen Levine
Jean Shinoda Bolen
Daniel Brown
Jack Engler
Margaret Brenman-Gibson
Joanna Macy

Parallax Press
Berkeley, California

Parallax Press
P.O. Box 7355
Berkeley, California 94707

Cover design by Gay Reineck. Text design by Ayelet Maida. Cover photographs and photographs throughout the text by Valerie Reed and N. Prasad. Author photo credits (pp. vii-xi): H.H. the Dalai Lama, Daniel Goleman, and Jack Engler by Valerie Reed and N. Prasad; Stephen Levine by William Abronowicz; Daniel Brown by Russell Backer; other photos courtesy of the authors.

This book is based on the October 1989 *Harmonia Mundi* conference held in Newport Beach, California, organized by Ronald W. Jue and the EastWest Foundation. Royalties will be donated to the Foundation for Universal Responsibility, established by H. H. the Dalai Lama in 1989 to promote the values of universal responsibility worldwide.

LIBRARY OF CONGRESS CATALOGING-IN-PUBLICATION DATA
Bstan— dzin-rgya-mtsho, Dalai Lama XIV, 1935-
   Worlds in harmony : dialogues on compassionate action
   His Holiness the Dalai Lama with Daniel Goleman ... [et al.].
      p.   cm.
   "Based on the October 1989 Harmonia Mundi conference held in Newport
Beach, California" — T.p. verso.
   ISBN 0-938077-77-5 : $12.50
   1. Buddhism —Psychology. 2. Psychotherapy—Religious aspects—
Buddhism. I. Goleman, Daniel. II. Title.
BQ4570.P76B78   1992
294.3'375—dc20   92-16826
                                                                    CIP

CONTENTS

ABOUT THE AUTHORS

His Holiness, Tenzin Gyatso, the Fourteenth Dalai Lama, has been the spiritual and temporal leader of Tibet since 1951, when he was sixteen years old. Since 1959, he has lived in exile in Dharamsala, India, teaching and practicing Buddhism, and serving as the head of the Tibetan government- in-exile. He travels worldwide, sharing  the teachings of Buddhism and working to preserve the educational, cultural, and religious institutions of Tibet. In 1989, the week of these dialogues, he was awarded the Nobel Peace Prize for his efforts to find a nonviolent solu- tion to the Tibetan quest for independence. He is the author of *Freedom in Exile; Kindness, Clarity and Insight; A Policy of Kindness; My Land and My People;* and many other books.

Jean Shinoda Bolen, M.D. is a psychia-
trist, Jungian analyst, and Clinical
Professor of Psychiatry at the Univer-
sity of California Medical Center, San
Francisco. She is author of *The Tao of
Psychology, Goddesses in Everywoman,
Gods in Everyman,* and *Ring of Power.*
A former Board member of the Ms.
Foundation for Women, she ap-

peared in the Academy Award Winning documentary
Women—for America, for the World and is engaged in explor-
ing and linking the archetypal and spiritual dimensions of
the women's movement, nuclear disarmament, and concern for the Earth.

Margaret Brenman-Gibson, Ph.D. is a
Clinical Professor of Psychiatry at
Cambridge Hospital, Harvard
Medical School; a Senior Consultant
in Research and Education at the
Austen Riggs Center; and a Senior
Research Associate at the Center for
Psychological Studies in the Nuclear
Age. Author of many books, she has
devoted the last two decades to the investigation of the
creative process; she is now focusing on the creative process
in weapons-makers at Livermore and Los Alamos Laborato-
ries. She has long combined her psychological expertise
with political activism, particularly through Physicians for
Social Responsibility.

Daniel Brown, Ph.D. is Director of a
Boston-area clinic for the treatment
of people traumatized by political oppression and torture. He is also Director of Behavioral Medicine Services at
Cambridge Hospital; Assistant Professor of Psychology, Harvard Medical
School; and Adjunct Professor,
Simmons School of Social Work. He
has spent twenty years investigating states of consciousness
from both Eastern and Western perspectives. He is co-
author of *Transformations of Consciousness* and *Human
Feelings* and translator of meditation texts from Tibetan
and Sanskrit.

 *Jack Engler, Ph.D.* is a training thera-
pist at Harvard Medical School and
has a private psychotherapy practice
in Cambridge, Massachusetts. He is a
leading thinker in developing the
relationship between psychoanalysis
and the psychology of classical
Buddhism. He is a past president of
the Board of Directors of the Insight
Meditation Society in Barre, Massachusetts, and a founder
of the new Barre Center for Buddhist Studies. With Daniel
Brown and Ken Wilber, he is co-author of *Transformations
of Consciousness.*

Daniel Goleman, Ph.D. is a psychologist and award-winning journalist, who reports on behavioral sciences for *The New York Times.* His areas of research and commentary include Asian psychological systems and relaxation techniques, meditation, and methods to reduce stress. He is a member of the Scientific Advisory  Board of the Mind/Body Medical Institute, a committee member of Tibet House, New York, and a founding member of the Mind and Life Research Network. He is author of *The Creative Spirit; Vital Lies, Simple Truths; The Meditative Mind;* and co-author of *Mind Science.* During these dialogues, he served as moderator.

 *Joanna Macy, Ph.D.* is a scholar of Buddhism, general systems theory, and deep ecology. Weaving these threads together, she leads workshops and trainings in many countries to empower creative, sustained social action. She is the author of *World as Lover, World as Self; Despair and Personal Power in the Nuclear Age; Dharma and Development;* and *Mutual Causality in Buddhism and General Systems Theory;* and co-author of *Thinking Like a Mountain.* She is a founder of the Nuclear Guardianship Project to monitor nuclear waste and is on the faculties of the California Institute of Integral Studies in San Francisco and the Starr King School for the Ministry in Berkeley.

Stephen Levine, poet and meditation teacher, is known internationally for his counseling on dying and bereavement. He and his wife Ondrea were directors of the Hanuman Foundation Dying Project He is the author of *A Gradual Awakening; Who Dies? An Investigation of Conscious Living and Conscious Dying; Meetings at the Edge; Healing into Life and Death; Guided Meditations: Exploration and Healings;* and co-author, with Ram Dass, of *Grist for the Mill.* He lives in the mountains of New Mexico, in the silence of the deep woods, and teaches just a few times each year.

Joel Edelman, J.D. is a mediator, lawyer, marriage and family counselor, holotropicbreathwork facilitator in Santa Monica, California. He practices and teaches dispute mediation within and between families, businesses, and international organizations. He is co-author of *Two to Make War, One to Make Peace: Preventing and Responding to Conflict in Love, Work and Life* (forthcoming). He was coordinator of the dialogues presented in *Worlds in Harmony* and organizer of the small group discussions. He also prepared and read the questions from the audience.

About the Translators

During these dialogues, H.H. the Dalai Lama spoke in both English and Tibetan. When he spoke Tibetan, his translators were Thubten Jinpa and B. Alan Wallace.

Thubten Jinpa, a student at Kings College, Cambridge University, England, was born in Zonghar, Tibet. He received his initial monastic training at Zonghar Chode Monastery, India. In 1978, he entered Shartse College of Ganden University, where he engaged in intensive study of Buddhist philosophy, epistemology, and logic. He received his Geshe degree in 1989 and has taught logic and philosophy. He is one of the principal interpreters for H.H. the Dalai Lama.

B. Alan Wallace is a graduate student in Religious Studies at Stanford University. He studied at the Library of Tibetan Works and Archives and the Buddhist School of Dialectics in Dharamsala, India, and at the Tibet Institute and Centre for Higher Tibetan Studies in Switzerland. He is author of *Choosing Reality: A Contemplative View of Physics and the Mind* and translator of several books on Tibetan Buddhism, language, and medicine. He is also Spiritual Director of the Dharma Friendship Foundation in Seattle.

EDITOR'S PREFACE

Worlds in Harmony is the fruit of an historic three-day
conference held in October 1989 in Newport Beach,
California. It developed from a wish expressed by His
Holiness the Dalai Lama to learn more about the Western
mind and the relationship between Buddhist and Western
psychology.

Through discussions among Lobsang Rapgay, former
Deputy Secretary in the private office of the Dalai Lama
and a student of Western psychology; Ronald Wong Jue,
past President of the Association for Transpersonal Psychology; and Daniel Goleman, a psychotherapist and editor on
behavioral sciences for *The New York Times*, the idea arose
for a public gathering to be sponsored by the EastWest
Foundation in which His Holiness and a panel of promi-
nent psychotherapists familiar with Buddhism could
exchange ideas and ask one another questions. When His
Holiness was invited to select the topics and format, he
deferred to the panelists, feeling that they would know best
what would be of interest to an American audience.

At least once a month for the eight months prior to the
conference, the panelists met with Ronald Jue, Lobsang
Rapgay, and Joel Edelman, the conference coordinator, in
person or by telephone, to create a meaningful format for

these dialogues. They wished to create an environment that would encourage the exploration of issues concerning Buddhism, psychology, and the bridge between personal consciousness and global concerns. To accomplish this, they established a number of criteria for the dialogues: that they be friendly and comfortable, yet challenging and even confrontational; that they be ongoing, not just a three-day "show"; that the audience be participants and not just observers; and that it be a true dialogue, not just questions posed to His Holiness. They also wanted the process of creating and conducting the conference to be congruent with its subject matter. It was decided to invite thirty-five skilled, small group facilitators.

In July, three months before the conference, several members of the planning committee met with the Dalai Lama in Santa Monica, California. His Holiness seemed delighted with the "unique format that would in itself create an environment for transformation to be possible." He said that he thought "the shift would take place for the participants more as a result of *their* participation in small groups than because of the on-stage, public dialogue."

Each morning and afternoon of the conference, there was an hour-and-a-half panel discussion. Then the nearly 1,000 members of the audience met in groups of around twenty-five to explore their reactions, responses, ideas, and questions. Following that, the group facilitators met to decide which questions to bring to the next dialogue of the panelists. The process of going back and forth between the small groups and the panel discussions worked remarkably well. His Holiness had been correct in predicting that this format would engage and transform the entire audience. As you will see, the dialogues were rich and energetic, and the questions from the audience enhanced them greatly. For two evenings following the dialogues, His Holiness gave public lectures on these same topics, and these appear in this book as the introduction, "Cultivating Altruism," and afterword, "Genuine Compassion."

It has been a great pleasure to help edit these dialogues. I especially wish to thank Miles Vich, Molly Maguire Silverman, Stephen Batchelor, Pat Aiello, Mark Waldman, Surya Das, Alan Wallace, Ronald Jue, Joel Edelman, and all of the panelists for their help.

Arnold Kotler
Berkeley, California
April 1992

ACKNOWLEDGMENTS

To the seven panelists—Daniel Goleman, Stephen Levine, Jean Shinoda Bolen, Daniel Brown, Jack Engler, Margaret Brenman-Gibson, and Joanna Macy, I express my most sincere thanks and appreciation. Dan Goleman, with great sensitivity to the ideological and cultural differences between East and West, provided the leadership for the group process, helped create balance in the selection of discussants, and skillfully guided the group in developing the dialogues. I want to extend special notes of appreciation to Joel Edelman, for handling the many important details of the program as conference coordinator, and Lobsang Rapgay, who brought to me the initial idea of a dialogue with His Holiness, for the many seminal discussions on Buddhism and psychotherapy that inspired the development of this program. I also wish to thank Larry Peters and the many others who helped with the conference; Miles Vich, whose encouragement provided the impetus for developing the transcripts into a book; Tom and Elizabeth Tierney, for their generosity in the early stages of the book; Arnold Kotler, for editing and polishing the transcripts; and Valerie Reed and N. Prasad, whose photographs captured the spirit of the conference. Most of all, my deepest gratitude goes to H.H. the Dalai Lama, whose life mirrors the spiritual qualities of compassion and wisdom and a deep commitment to the promotion of these values in our global society. Just a few hours after these dialogues were completed, it was announced that His Holiness had been awarded the Nobel Peace Prize for 1989.

Ronald Wong Jue, Ph.D.
Newport Beach, California
May 1992

Daniel Goleman

The generation now alive is the first in human history to glimpse the possibility of the end of nature, the end of our world. We live in a planet that can die. *The Bulletin of Atomic Scientists* has a clock on its cover that tracks how close we are to the final hour, and that clock has been close to midnight for many decades. For a long time it was because of the nuclear peril; now it is also because of the ecological peril—the spreading of deserts, the pollution of air and water, the heating of the planet, the world's trees being felled at acres per minute, and on and on. What we are doing to the planet now is no different from what we have been doing to humanity for some time.

We produce more food today than ever before in human history, yet more people are starving than ever before. There is a greater concentration of wealth than ever, and yet the gap between rich and poor is greater than ever before. Democracy is spreading throughout the globe, and yet some of the most oppressive regimes in history are thriving. And in this century we have seen the worst genocides of history: the holocaust of World War II, a million Cambodians killed by the Khmer Rouge, and many millions killed by both Stalin and Mao, including one million Tibetans.

With the advent of instantaneous communication, we are left with no room for excuses. We are able to see the poverty and disease, the hunger and oppression, the growth of deserts, and the shrinking of forests. We see all too clearly the suffering, both individual and planetary. Ours is a world out of harmony. That was the occasion for these dialogues.

The Dalai Lama represents the one great culture centered on a wisdom tradition to survive intact into modern times. And the fragility of our times is demonstrated by the fact that even that culture survives fully intact only in exile. Tibet represents a time capsule of sorts for the modern world from an age when life was centered on the spirit and the world was in harmony, when the inner sciences—the art of being—were developed to the highest levels. At a time when the modern world is adrift and in crisis, we need more than ever to bring this wisdom to bear.

Science and technology have brought immense control over nature, but power without wisdom is dangerous. We need to balance our modern capabilities with an ancient wisdom. His Holiness the Dalai Lama often speaks of the interconnectedness of all things. In a sense, that means we are all in this together. He has said, also, that just because these times are so dire, it is a great honor to be alive now, at this moment, on this planet. It is we who bear the responsibility, who face the challenge, who must take care of the planet, not just for ourselves, but for the future, for our children.

During three days of October 1989 in Newport Beach, California, the Dalai Lama joined seven renowned helping professionals—psychotherapists, those who work with the dying, and others—for an engaging dialogue on the nature of suffering and the ways that wise and compassionate action can help overcome the suffering of our day. The dialogue involved everyone in the hall, nearly 1,000 people, through small group discussions and questions from the audience. The voices recorded in this book are just an expression of all of our common concerns.

WORLDS IN HARMONY

Dialogues on Compassionate Action

INTRODUCTION: CULTIVATING ALTRUISM

H.H. the Dalai Lama

Compassion, love, and altruism are not just religious qualities. As human beings, and even as animals, we need compassion and affection to develop, sustain ourselves, and survive. Even before we were born, when we were still in the womb, our mother's calmness was very much related with ours. Then, during the first few weeks after birth, a very crucial period for our development, even such simple things as our mother's touch were very important in developing our brain. For the next few years, without the kindness or affection of our parent or someone else, we could not have survived. Now, as adults, we still need someone we can trust, someone from whom we can receive affection; and when we become old, we will again be heavily dependent on others for affection. This is the human way of life.

Our future depends on the younger generation. In order to develop a generation of healthy human beings, it is important to offer them a compassionate environment when they are still small. It is easy to recognize children whose parents, for various reasons, have neglected them, and who, as a result, have a helpless, insecure feeling. Their minds are always agitated, and, in fact, their whole lives are somehow ruined. In a healthy family, where children receive consistent affection and protection, the children are very happy and develop self-confidence. As a result, their health is better and their lives become something of value. Compassion and affection are crucial for this.

What is the purpose of life? I believe that satisfaction, joy, and happiness are the ultimate purposes of life. And the basic sources of happiness are a good heart, compassion, and love. If we have these mental attitudes, even if we are surrounded by hostility, we will feel little disturbance. On the other hand, if we lack compassion and our mental state is filled with anger or hatred, no matter what the situation, we will not have peace. Without compassion, we feel insecure, and, eventually, we will feel fear and a lack of self-confidence. Then even something small can destabilize our inner world. But if we are calm, even if we are confronted by a serious problem, we will know how to handle it.

In order to utilize human intelligence fully, we need calmness. If we lose our stability through anger, it becomes difficult to use our intelligence well. If we are unstable and influenced by negative thoughts, our intelligence will be used wrongly. Looking at human history over the last few thousand years, and particularly in this century, we see that human tragedies like the holocaust arise from negative emotions such as hatred, anger, fear, and suspicion. And we also see that the many positive developments of human history have all come from good mental states, such as compassion.

In the modern economy, every nation is dependent on every other nation. Even hostile nations must cooperate in economics and in the use of the world's resources. So, in both the global reality and the situation in the family, human beings need harmony and cooperation. Genuine cooperation comes not through force, but through mutual respect. An altruistic attitude is the most crucial factor.

If an individual has a sense of responsibility for humanity, he or she will naturally take care of the environment, including the slowing down of industrial growth and population growth. If we think narrow-mindedly and see only our own surroundings, we will not create a positive future. In the past, when we neglected the long-term consequences of our actions, it was less serious. But today, through science and technology, we can create far greater benefits or much more damage. The threat of nuclear weapons and the ability to damage our environment through, for example, deforestation, pollution, and ozone layer depletion, are quite alarming. We can all see the dangers of potential tragedies here. But other, barely noticeable changes, such as the loss of natural resources like topsoil, may be even more dangerous because, by the time they begin to affect us, it will be too late. Therefore, in all respects, we see that genuine cooperation, the real sense of responsibility based on compassion and altruism, require not only that we respect human beings, but also that we respect, take care of, and refrain from interfering with other species and the environment. On every level of work concerning the happiness or satisfaction of the individual, the family, the nation, and the international community, the key is the altruistic mind.

As I travel around the world and meet people from various walks of life, I see that many are now showing real concern about these matters and agree with the views I am expressing. The fundamental question is how can we develop and maintain compassion. Certain religious beliefs, if you have them, are very helpful; but if you do not have them, you can also survive quite happily. Compassion, love, and forgiveness, however, are not luxuries. They are fundamental for our survival.

Whenever I speak about the importance of compassion and love, people ask me what is the method for developing them? This is not easy. I don't think there is any particular package or method that enables you to develop these qualities instantaneously. You cannot just press a button and wait for them to appear. I know that many people expect things like this from a Dalai Lama, but, really, all I have to offer is my own experience. If you find something useful in this, I hope you will use it. But if you don't find much of interest, I don't mind if you just leave it.

I think we must begin by investigating our own daily experience and reading stories about our neighbors to see the consequences of anger and the consequences of love and compassion. If we make a comparative study of these two attitudes, we will develop a deeper understanding of the negative results of anger and the positive results of compassion. Once we are convinced of the benefits of compassion and the negative consequences of anger and hatred—that they always cause unhappiness within us— then we will make more effort to have less anger. We will take a more cautious approach. We usually think that anger is protecting us from something, but that is a deception. So, most important is to realize the negative consequences of anger and hatred. I have seen that negative emotions do not help at all.

Sometimes people feel that when there is a natural disaster, or a tragedy brought about by human beings, we will have more energy and boldness to fight back if we are angry. But, in my experience, even though anger gives us

energy to act or to speak out, it is blind energy, and difficult to control. During that moment we may not care, but,
after a few minutes, we will feel much regret. When we are
angry, we use nasty or harsh words, which, once spoken,
cannot be withdrawn. Afterwards, when our anger has
disappeared and we meet the other person again, we feel
terrible. During that moment, we lost our judgment and
became half-mad. There are many different levels and
forces of anger. When a small anger is about to arise, it is
easy to control. But, if a stronger, more forceful anger
comes, we have to try different techniques to handle it.
Once we see negative mental states as negative, that alone
will reduce their strength.

I come from the northeastern part of Tibet. Usually,
people from that area are quite short-tempered. So if I get
angry, I can use this as an excuse. When I was fifteen or
twenty, I was quite short-tempered, but through Buddhist
training and through difficult experiences, I have been
able to improve my mental stability. Difficult experiences
are very good training for the mind. They help us develop
a kind of inner determination.

Today, compared with twenty or thirty years ago, my
mental stability is much better. Of course, irritation still
arises sometimes, but it disappears quickly, and heated
agitation is almost never there. As a result, I experience
more happiness and joy. When the worst news comes, I feel
uncomfortable for a few minutes, but afterward, I don't
feel much disturbance. Through training, we can change.
We can improve ourselves. As a result of training, my
mental state remains comparatively calm. I am usually in a
relaxed mood, and my health has been good—I never use
sleeping pills, and appetite is not a problem. Through my

own experience, I am convinced that as a result of less anger, we become happier and healthier, smile and laugh more, and have more friends.

Human intelligence is one of our best attributes. It can assess the long and short-term consequences of our actions. But it cannot function properly when we are under the sway of a strong emotion. When we react in anger, we do not know whether our action will be effective or not. But, without anger, we can analyze the situation and see whether a strong counter-measure is called for, and, if it is, we can take such an action with no ill-feeling. If we have a genuine sense of universal responsibility, we are also concerned about the other person and his or her long-term consequences. With this realization, we see that a counter-measure that is taken without anger is more correct and more effective. The only usefulness of anger is the energy it brings, but we can also derive energy from other sources without having to cause harm to ourselves or others.

We identify someone who directly or indirectly harms us as our "enemy." Generally, we don't like our enemy—that is the definition of enemy. We usually see our so-called enemy as external, such as a group or an individual who can damage our property, hurt our friends, or even take our life. But if we undertake a deeper investigation, we see that these three things—property, friends, and our own bodies—are not 100% sources of happiness for us. Sometimes because of our property, we experience more sadness; because of our friends, we get into trouble; and because of our bodies, we have more pain. Even though these things are supposed to be sources of happiness for us, we cannot be sure. We might say they are 70 or 80% sources of happiness, but certainly not 100%.

On the other hand, mental tranquility, or calmness, is a very important source of happiness. It is almost certain that if you have mental calmness, joy will arise. An external enemy, no matter how powerful, cannot strike directly at our mental calmness, because calmness is formless. This ultimate source of happiness or joy can only be destroyed by our own anger. So the real enemy, the real destroyer of joy, is anger.

Thinking along these lines is a kind of experiment or scientific investigation. When scientists investigate matter, if they find something useful, they will cultivate it, and if they find something harmful or poisonous, they will avoid it. It is the same with mind. There are many different minds, different thoughts, and different states of mind, and each directly affects our happiness. When we examine different states of mind within ourselves, we can cultivate and develop those that are positive and beneficial and avoid and eliminate those that are negative and destructive. The basic difference between the investigation of external matter and the investigation of mind is that the former requires large laboratories, complex missions, and a huge budget. In the internal world, you just investigate which thoughts are useful and which ones are harmful, and you keep and develop the ones you like, making effort constantly. Over time, your mental state will become much better balanced, and you will find that you are much happier and more stable. This is a kind of yoga for the mind. It is very worthwhile and so simple.

The smile is one of the most beautiful characteristics of a human being. Not many other animals smile. I recently visited Sea World and saw animals with a lot of intelligence and some closeness toward human beings, but no smiles.

There are two types of smiles—genuine and artificial. If our smile is genuine and sincere, arising out of compassion, or altruism, it gives us comfort.

Each day when we wake up, we can say to ourselves, "Altruistic attitude." If we have an altruistic attitude, many favorable things will come. But if we wake up with anger, hatred, or jealousy, these negative emotions will force us to spend the whole day feeling suspicious and uncomfortable. If we sincerely investigate and analyze these things, according to our own experiences and what our neighbors tell us about their daily lives, we will slowly gain stability and, with that, the ability to notice the moment a negative emotion is about to arise.

I practice these things and I know they are helpful. I try to be sincere to everyone, even the Chinese. If I develop some kind of ill-will, anger, or hatred, who will lose? I will lose my happiness, my sleep, and my appetite, but my ill feelings won't hurt the Chinese at all. If I am agitated, my physical condition will become weak, and some people I could make happy will not become happy.

Some people may criticize me, but I try to remain joyful. If we want to work effectively for freedom and justice, it is best to do so without anger or ill-will. If we feel calm and have a sincere motivation, we can work hard for thirty or forty years. I believe that because of my firm commitment to nonviolence, based on a genuine sense of brotherhood and sisterhood, some positive results have been produced.

1

The Nature of Suffering

Joanna Macy: Your Holiness, Daniel Goleman, in his beautiful and sobering introductory remarks, reminds us of the condition of our world. He points out that we are extremely close to the final hour for the human race and for our brother and sister species as well. This is a time of great danger, and it requires an immediate and massive response from us.

In my own work, I find that there are many different kinds of responses to the suffering of the world. Many people who want to be compassionate are aware of, but somehow don't believe, the extent of the problem. The facts are just too painful and overwhelming to face, so they continue with business-as-usual and rarely speak with their family or friends about the suffering of our world. People seem to take refuge in two kinds of hope: that things will work out because of our great technological know-how, and that, if we are peaceful and good in our hearts, everything will be all right. My question, Your Holiness, is whether these kinds of hope tend to keep us from facing what we need to face. Can hope give us false comfort and keep us from doing what we need to do?

Dalai Lama: If "hope" is what prevents us from seeing the true state of things, that is a problem. But, you know, I generally consider hope to be quite important. Whether we achieve what we are hoping for or not, it is important for us to keep hope. Hope is the basis of our future, the basis of success. If we remain hopeful, with an optimistic attitude, it can help relieve many of our anxieties.

When I look at the global situation today, I find many reasons to be hopeful. Because of the threat of a nuclear holocaust, more and more people realize that resolving conflicts through war is totally unacceptable. Despite the different ideologies and economic systems, many people are trying to avoid war and achieve coexistence, and I think that the desire for peace has greatly increased. In the last few years, I have met a number of physicists who made significant contributions to the discovery of nuclear weapons who are now showing a deep concern about peace. Because of technology, communications are much improved, and, as a result, our interrelations are also improved. Such concepts as "nation" and "continent" have become less significant. In Europe, many young people— German, Italian, and French—realize that they are interlinked.

Another thing we are seeing today is the dissolution of totalitarian systems. Human beings want freedom, more space to move. Even animals want that. The result of the human desire for liberty is the movement for democracy, not only in Eastern Europe, but also in places like the Philippines, Palestine, and Latin America. To me, this shows that the basic human spirit is gaining the upper hand, and this is a hopeful sign.

Until the early part of this century, people consumed the world's resources as if they were limitless. No one was seriously concerned about the planet. Today, there are even political parties whose ideologies are based on pre-serving the environment. Because of increased human knowledge, we have been able to reach a deeper level. The long-term consequences of our acts have become clearer, and more and more people are showing deep concern about the natural environment. This is also very positive.

For centuries, people in the West regarded material and spiritual concerns as entirely separate. Today, I meet many people who realize that this is not so. They understand that there is no point in neglecting our inner feelings or experiences. Even though much of modern science is still very remote, it is we human beings who created it in order to benefit ourselves. But sometimes we become too excited about the technology and forget about humanity, and today this limitation is revealing itself. We see that through science and material accomplishment alone, it is impos-sible to get complete satisfaction. Satisfaction must come from within. The fact that we are returning to our basic sense of humanity is a positive, healthy development. So I have many reasons to be hopeful, rather than pessimistic.

But ultimately we must remember that hope is just hope. Unless hope leads to action, it is not of much use. Although I myself pray, frankly speaking I'm not much of a believer in prayer. Action is much more important than simply praying. Unless our insights result in some practical action, they are not useful at all. The real effect must come through action and not just hope.

Joanna Macy: As people begin to act on whatever problem they feel drawn to—toxic wastes, animal experimentation, or other issues—they often discover that the suffering is even greater than they had expected. Your Holiness, can you suggest spiritual and mental practices to help us look directly at the suffering and not turn away from it?

Dalai Lama: The attitude we have towards the suffering matters a lot. If we look at it from too close up, we may feel overwhelmed, so that on top of the suffering itself, we also have depression and anxiety. But if we look at the same situation from a different perspective, we may be able to see that although it is truly tragic, it could be worse. Looking in this way reduces the level of our anxiety and suffering. In each event, there are a number of aspects. If we look at just one negative aspect, we will think only about that, and we may be overwhelmed.

In Buddhism, we do not deny or avoid suffering. Instead, we concentrate on it, using a kind of analytical meditation. For example, if someone harms us, if we look at that person only as someone who has caused us harm, our anger may be overwhelming. But if we look at her from the angle of something wonderful she did in the past, we will have another perspective, and it will not be too difficult to practice patience and develop the inner strength needed to overcome our negative feeling. That unfortunate event can actually help us increase our own inner strength, and seeing that can reduce our feeling of negativity towards the other person.

Analyzing the situation in this way is called "penetrating it." If you want to deny or avoid something and have a picnic or a vacation instead, you may feel some short-term relief, but the problem will remain. So instead of doing that, if you penetrate into the suffering or the tragedy and see its nature with some perspective, your mental attitude will improve, and you will have a real chance of resolving the problem.

Margaret Brenman-Gibson: Gandhi said, "We must not think of the one who does harm as an evil person; we must think of him or her as having done a harmful or evil action, but there is always another chance."

Dalai Lama: Yes, that is very important. It is important to make this distinction between the act and the actor, not simply to identify the actor as 100% negative.

So, if you want to lessen some suffering, you can withdraw your mind from it, or you can investigate and penetrate it. You mention animal experimentation. From the Buddhist point of view, all sentient beings—beings who have feelings, experiences, and sensations—are regarded as equal, so the idea of gaining benefit for one living being by sacrificing another is not something we can condone. But there may be an exceptional case where, in order to save an entire species or to save a being who has the possibility of creating more happiness for a larger community of beings, you might have to sacrifice the life of another who has less ability to create such opportunities for happiness. There could be a case where, in order to bring about new ways of treating a human illness, you might be confronted with a situation in which you cannot avoid subjecting certain animals to laboratory experiments. If you are in such a circumstance, there are two ways you might deal with the suffering you are causing: to totally ignore the sensations and feelings of the animals, or to try to maintain awareness of the animal's suffering while also bearing in mind the long-term benefit the experiment can produce. If you have to be involved in such an experiment, working in this second way can reduce your anxieties. If we compare the two ways of dealing with the problem, being aware of both the pain and the benefits of this experiment is far better than ignoring the suffering of the animal. This does not justify sacrificing an animal, but it may be a better way to perform an experiment than to neglect the sensations and pain of the animal.

Margaret Brenman-Gibson: When you say that for the greater benefit of human beings, it is perhaps all right to sacrifice certain animals, it seems to me we are on very thin ice. Who is to decide for the greater benefit of whom?

Dalai Lama: Yes, I agree. It is a very delicate question. The logic is that in order to save many, you may have to sacrifice one. That may be more correct than to sacrifice many in order to save only one. But the best way is to avoid experimenting on animals.

Still, in exceptional cases, you may have to sacrifice the life of an animal in an experiment in order to save human lives. According to the logic I have proposed, because human beings have a greater potential to serve more living beings, under certain circumstances it may be understandable to conduct such an experiment.

Daniel Brown: Your Holiness, I am concerned that saying it is sometimes permissible to inflict harm and suffering on others for the greater good can easily be misused. For example, in many countries people are disappeared, tortured, and sometimes killed. If you interview the tortur-ers, they will often tell you that they did not see anything wrong with their action, because they were doing it for the greater good of their political group. There is an errone-ous view there because it is not for the greater good of humanity, but just to keep one group in power. These people seem to have a sincere conviction that what they are doing is for the greater good. My question to you is: how do you balance this altruistic wish with some correct view or wisdom?

Dalai Lama: That kind of misconception stems from ignorance. The best way to overcome it is to develop altruism based on wisdom. To sacrifice one for the benefit of many may, theoretically speaking, be correct, but to implement it is very complicated. We must analyze the situation carefully, and often it is very difficult to be sure what to do. Sometimes the situation is so complex that it requires a kind of clairvoyance to see how to proceed. The safest way is to try to prevent such situations from arising.

Margaret Brenman-Gibson: Dan Brown's question reminds me of something my teacher, Erik Homburger Erikson, said frequently: "We treat other nations and peoples as if they were members of another species, and then we feel that it is all right to kill them for our so-called betterment."

During the Vietnam War, it was frequently said that we were there to liberate the Vietnamese, even as we were dropping tons of TNT on them. When Daniel Ellsberg, originally working for the government as a "cold warrior," went to Vietnam, he came to the point of realizing that they were not of another species, and he said, "The Vietnamese people became as familiar to me as my own hands." Soon, prosecuting the war became impossible for him.

Because of his empathy—feeling the other creature's feeling, whether it is an animal or a person—he could no longer live in the same way, and he had to resist, to end not only his personal role but the role of the United States government in that wrongful war. This was when he put out the truth about the war, in the celebrated *Pentagon Papers*. Empathy is a basis for a transformation of consciousness, for not turning away from suffering. When you see and feel that "you are me, and I am you," you can no longer turn away from the suffering, and you must resist the wrongful action. Wouldn't you agree, Your Holiness, that when we see other people as somehow being of another species, different from ourselves, we are liable to think that we have the right to harm them or even to kill them?

Dalai Lama: This is very true, I totally agree. There is a quotation in a Buddhist sutra that says, "Reflect on your own feelings and sensations, and then see others as the same." Basically, every being is the same. Every being has the right to be happy and to overcome suffering. There is a close connection between oneself and others. Our own survival depends entirely on others. Therefore, showing concern about others ultimately brings benefit to us.

In reality, we have to live together. We cannot destroy all the other beings. Even if we do not like our neighbor, we have to live together. In the field of economics, also, we have to depend on others, even hostile nations. That is a reality. Under these circumstances, it is always better to live harmoniously, in a friendly way, than to maintain a negative attitude. The globe is becoming much smaller and more interdependent. Empathy and altruism are the keys for true happiness.

Margaret Brenman-Gibson: And for the survival of the planet.

Dalai Lama: Yes. And altruism is more than just a feeling of sympathy. It includes a sense of responsibility, of taking care of one another. When we consider the other as someone precious and respected, it is natural that we will help them and share with them as expressions of our love. According to many scientists, we need affection for our brains to develop properly. This shows that our very nature is involved with affection, love, and compassion.

Joanna Macy: Your Holiness, I would like to ask you about another situation in which animals suffer a lot—factory farms. In order to change that practice, to reduce the suffering of these fellow species, we need to see their pain. But for many of us, it seems to be too much to bear, and we want to look away. You have described the practice of not turning away from pain, but penetrating into it so that we are not afraid of it. Can you speak more about it, especially in relation to our animal brothers and sisters who are being tortured?

Dalai Lama: Thousands—millions and billions—of animals are killed for food. That is very sad. We human beings can live without meat, especially in our modern world. We have a great variety of vegetables and other supplementary foods, so we have the capacity and the responsibility to save billions of lives. I have seen many individuals and groups promoting animal rights and following a vegetarian diet. This is excellent.

Certain killing is purely a "luxury." Hunting and fishing as sports, for example, are just nonsense. But other killing, for example commercial fishing for eating, is more understandable. But perhaps the saddest is factory farming. The poor animals there really suffer. I once visited a poultry farm in Japan where they keep 200,000 hens for two years just for their eggs. During those two years, they are prisoners. Then after two years, when they are no longer productive, the hens are sold. That is really shocking, really sad. We must support those who are attempting to reduce that kind of unfair treatment.

An Indian friend told me that his young daughter has been arguing with him that it is better to serve one cow to ten people than to serve chicken or other small animals, since more lives would be involved. In the Indian tradition, beef is always avoided, but I think there is some logic to her argument. Shrimp, for example, are very small. For one plate, many lives must be sacrificed. To me, this is not at all delicious. I find it really awful, and I think it is better to avoid these things. If your body needs meat, it may be better to eat bigger animals. Eventually you may be able to eliminate the need for meat. I think that our basic nature as human beings is to be vegetarian—making every effort not to harm other living beings. If we apply our intelligence, we can create a sound, nutritional program.

It is very dangerous to ignore the suffering of any sentient being. Even in warfare, it is better to be aware of the suffering of others and our own discomfort for causing them pain. Warfare is killing. It is 100% negative. The way it is mechanized today is even worse. Where warfare remains "humanized, " I mean where it remains in touch with true human feelings, it is much safer. When the warrior forgets about the suffering of others in order to achieve some small benefit, that is really dangerous. I am thinking here of some Tibetan butchers. Although they make their livelihood as butchers, at the same time they show kindness and love towards the animals. Before the slaughter, they give the animal some pills, and after they finish, they say a prayer. Although it is still killing, I think it is better with that kind of feeling.

Daniel Brown: Your Holiness, I have a question concerning people who have suffered extreme abuse, such as sexual or physical abuse as children, or the victims of atrocities like the holocausts in Germany, Central America, or Cambodia.

For example, we can take a specific instance of political torture. Consider the case of a man who, in his country-of-origin, was a small farmer. He was actively and genuinely concerned to help the poor, and worked against oppression by trying to reform the laws about distribution of land and wealth in his country. In the course of doing that, he was "disappeared" and tortured. The torture consisted of being taken away from his family and blindfolded. He was then submitted to numerous beatings and was submerged in water with excrement. Various electrical shocks were applied to his body, and he was hung from his hands and ankles like a helicopter, spun around and around, and then beaten. This continued for about six months. He was released and then went back to his work helping his people, although he had many nightmares and was highly anxious. Because he did not stop helping his people, two of his five children were murdered.

Finally, he left his country and sought refuge in the U.S., and he tried to continue to help his people from here. But he felt that by leaving and not carrying on that fight for his people directly in his native country, he had somehow let his people down. Finally he overcame his despair and continued, and then he learned that his other three children had been murdered, in an attempt to demoralize him. As a result he got severely depressed, sometimes suicidal, and panicky. Yet, the people who work with him try and help him continue his lifework of helping his people.

When I hear a story like this, and I hear many similar stories, I have a very strong reaction to the overwhelming suffering of someone with good intentions. How would one view that suffering from a Buddhist perspective? It seems to me that in Buddhism, the emphasis on suffering is on how the Three Poisons—clinging, aversion, and ignorance—contribute to the suffering of the ordinary mind. It seems to me that Western psychotherapists who work with trauma survivors emphasize the physical and social reality of such intense pain and suffering that is inflicted willfully and intentionally to destroy the dignity and humanity of another person, and to prevent them from helping oppressed people. From the perspective of ultimate truth, is this kind of suffering merely an illusion because we fail to understand suffering properly? I don't understand this, and I would like some way to know how one can view such a case of intense suffering and reconcile that with Buddhist notions of emptiness. Is such suffering merely illusion?

Dalai Lama: There are two levels and meanings of "illusion": In the conventional, or normal, level, your mind is simply confused, and you perceive incorrectly because of it. When you confront someone who has undergone a traumatic experience, this is real suffering. It is not just an illusion. In the situation you describe, there is real suffering and you have a correct perception of it.

There is another level of illusion that is far more subtle, that does not have to do with this level of confusion at all. On that level, you would say yes, because these are dependently related events, there is an illusory aspect to the suffering. But the chance of misunderstanding here is great. The true meaning of "emptiness" is the absence of independent existence. Usually, we project an independent existence onto events and things. "Emptiness" has a connotation of "fullness," of being dependent upon other factors. There is interconnectedness implied in the doctrine of emptiness. What is meant in Buddhism, particularly Madhyamika philosophy, by the term "illusion" is that phenomena do not exist independently of other phenomena, that their appearance of independent existence is illusory. This is all that is meant by "illusion," not that something is not really there.

Audience Question: Your Holiness, do you think that suffering is inevitable, or is it something that we ourselves create by seeing the world dualistically? Can some good come out of suffering?

Dalai Lama: In the Buddhist teachings, suffering is spoken of at three different levels. The first is blatant physical and mental pain, the second is the discontent associated with the fact that our pleasure and happiness will change into something else, and the third is the pervasive suffering of conditioned existence. All of these have one positive aspect. By being aware of the suffering, we can be inspired to be free of it. But the three kinds of suffering by themselves are not desirable. In fact, they are totally undesirable.

Margaret Brenman-Gibson: Suffering has always been part of the sentient condition, but we now live in a time when it is possible for humanity to wipe itself out entirely. The decisions that are being made today by the people who hold the power of the world in their hands—and they are mostly men—allow for the possibility of a level of suffering that has never been known before. Indeed, it is unprecedented in history that the instruments of warfare which have always brought suffering have a new and awesome potential in this nuclear age: namely to bring to an end the future human enterprise and, some think, all life on Earth. Under these circumstances, is suffering something we must accept as part of existence?

Dalai Lama: We can distinguish between man-made suffering and other suffering. If we adopt certain attitudes, we can definitely reduce man-made suffering. The other type of suffering, that is difficult to say. I think it depends on individual faith and individual practice.

Audience Question: How can we distinguish between another person's real suffering and projecting our own suffering onto other people?

Margaret Brenman-Gibson: If I feel a person is suffering about something, I usually say what I think, and I believe I can usually tell by their response whether I am reading something into their feelings or whether they are saying, "You're right. Let me tell you of my pain." I find this guideline useful, as a therapist.

Daniel Brown: It seems to me that it depends on our level of awareness. With an ordinary mind of ignorance, we may think we perceive suffering out there, when really it is our own fantasy.

In the Western psychotherapy traditions, there are methods that people use to make the distinction. They learn to gain a greater analytical knowledge of their own feelings or fantasies, and they are taught to discriminate more clearly between when it is their own fantasy or feeling and when it pertains to the suffering of the other person. In this country, this kind of learning occurs in good clinical practice, and it requires a certain level of awareness.

But it seems to me that from Buddhist practices we learn another level of awareness: the direct experience of co-dependent origination, of everything being inter-connected in some way. From that direct experience, we see how our thoughts and actions ripple out and affect everything else. Then, when we perceive suffering in a person or a group, we know that it affects their conscious-ness and ripples out in all directions, and that that causes a great disturbance. If it's a kind of abuse, we cannot fail to be affected by it. When someone has a direct experience of interconnection, the question of the difference between fantasizing about or projecting suffering and the reality of the person suffering just does not occur. We *must* be affected, because everything is interconnected.

Dalai Lama: Still, there is a distinction between one person's consciousness and that of another. They do not simply merge together.

Joanna Macy: A related question is, "Am I feeling my own pain, or am I feeling the world's pain?" I find that we really cannot separate the two. When we see the suffering of our brothers and sisters of other countries or the suffering of other species, we see how we are interconnected, how we are part of the culture that is doing that. As we were walking in here, Stephen was saying, "I am fatigued in a different way than I was when working with the dying, because for the last few years Ondrea and I have been working with sexually-abused women as well."

Jean Shinoda Bolen: How is it that people like us inflict pain on another human being? How could a person like me do such an awful thing to another person like me? It seems as if there is some pleasure in our culture in having and expressing power, which unfortunately often has to do with inflicting pain on others. This seems to be in the area of man-made, or human-made pain, which His Holiness was describing as unnecessary suffering.

Joanna Macy: Stephen himself was feeling this pain. Is it his pain or the women's pain?

Stephen Levine: If there is a place in me that the pain can stick to, it will. When we were working with people who were dying, I did not feel much resistance. People die, it is natural. Even the pain is natural. But when we started to work with people who had been abused and sometimes tortured, experiencing that somebody's heart, somebody's mind could be so closed, so insensitive, that they could inflict this suffering on another, I found myself becoming

27

sad and tired, and the pain stuck to me more. The places in me that fought injustice, that struggled with this lineage of pain, with this conspiracy of suffering in which we are all involved, that place within that is "kindly bent to ease us," had some difficulty straightening up. It stuck more when there was someone willing, even intending, to hurt another.

But slowly I came to recognize the difference between pain and suffering. Pain is a given. Born into a body with a nervous system, that nerve-net catches pain. When we bump into something, the body hurts. Born into a mind capable of accepting conflicting conditioning, the mind burns. I see that suffering and pain are not synonymous. Your Holiness, is suffering our response to pain? Could one just live in the pain, both physical and emotional, and not be suffering?

Dalai Lama: If by "pain" you mean physical sensations and by "suffering" you mean the mental responses that follow, then you can say that mental suffering and mental happiness are more acutely felt than physical pleasure or pain. Therefore, it is possible for the force of mental pleasure or mental suffering to overwhelm physical sensations.

To answer your question whether it is possible, in spite of experiencing pain, to avoid suffering, the answer is definitely yes. Sometimes we voluntarily accept a certain amount of physical pain. For example, in order to have a healthy body, we need to exercise. During those moments, we may feel tired and even feel some pain in our joints. But there are reasons to accept these pains, so mentally we have no suffering at all. Later, when we see our muscles grow, we even feel happy.

Audience Question: When someone's suffering spills over onto us, when a person physically or psychologically, consciously or unconsciously inflicts their suffering on us or demands something unreasonable of us, should we do what they say, try to forgive them, or stop them?

Dalai Lama: Until now I have been talking about how to change your mental attitude towards suffering, how to view it. If you do that with equanimity and calmness of mind, first of all, the suffering of the mind will decrease. You will not just react negatively. But after that, whether you let another person continue to behave in the same way depends on the situation. You have to judge each situation on an individual basis. Forgiveness, or patience, does not mean that you completely give in to anything anyone does to you.

Margaret Brenman-Gibson: What is the alternative?

Dalai Lama: If you are a tolerant person and another person is demanding something unreasonable, you may, without anger or ill-will, judge the situation and see if you need a counter-measure. Then you take the counter-measure. In the case of Tibet, there is a lot of suffering under the name of liberation. But if I see the Chinese leaders as human beings—our neighbors, people with a long history and a high civilization—instead of having ill-will, I have respect. Doing this helps reduce negative feelings and gives rise to patience and tolerance. This does not mean that I accept Chinese oppression. I do whatever I can to stand firm against oppression, but I do it without ill-will. In the case of an individual, it is quite similar. If there is an unreasonable demand on you, it may require some resistance or counter-measure. But that counter-measure will be more effective if it is not motivated by anger. When your mind is dominated by anger, you become half-mad, and you won't be able to hit the target.

Jean Shinoda Bolen: Your Holiness, Tibet was invaded, people were killed and raped, and many other awful things happened. As psychotherapists and as human beings, we always wonder how people can bear this and go on feeling joyful, and go on being active in the world to change the situation. Somehow I have the impression that you have managed to do that, that you are not obsessed by anger, fear, or hostility, and you continue to actively represent your people in the world. I wonder if you could tell us how you personally dealt with the awfulness of what you saw and experienced.

Dalai Lama: Perhaps it is the Tibetan personality. I think that it is natural for Tibetans to face adversity and tragedy in this way. I don't know if this is due to the influence of Buddhism or not. Tibet is a very large country with a very low population density. In this kind of situation, it is natural to look upon your neighbor as a person to help and from whom to receive help. When you live in a densely populated area, there may be a natural tendency to look upon your neighbor with suspicion and competitiveness and to withdraw from that person. There was a great feeling of space in Tibet. Given this and also the Buddhist influence, there is a kind of resilience among Tibetans.

Through Buddhist training, one develops an understanding of different levels of suffering. We also accept the theory of karma, or action, and that is also useful to lessen the mental suffering. When things have already happened, there is no use to worry. If we do our best, with sincere motivation, we feel very good if we have success, but if we do not, there is no regret. This kind of analytical attitude helps a lot.

Jean Shinoda Bolen: It also seems to me that as we get older, we get wiser, and we realize that, "This, too, shall pass." As we come to have an awareness of our previous lives, it is easier to be able to detach or forgive, because we realize that this is just one event in a series of historical events. Our perspective becomes a long historical view of things. Your Holiness, how much should we try to change the world to make it different?

Dalai Lama: In Buddhism, we do believe in life after death and the theory of karma, the law of action and its effects. These beliefs do contribute to a kind of equanimity towards your development and acceptance of things as they unfold. This may seem too simple, but speaking from a Buddhist point of view, as a monk, all of these problems can be attributed to a lack of altruism, compassion, sense of responsibility, or genuine sense of brotherhood and sisterhood. When you consider one thing superior, whenever the opportunity is there, you will exploit the thing you consider inferior.

Margaret Brenman-Gibson: Is there any use in trying to change this?

Dalai Lama: Of course. Through education, media, family life, and other means, we must introduce and bring to deeper awareness—if not for our present generation, for the future generations—the necessity of this altruistic mind and attitude. In order to awaken the future generation's mind to these issues, it is important to present them as questions of survival, not matters of religion or morality. Pain is unfortunate, but sometimes it can be an important factor to help people wake up, to realize that something is wrong.

As we gain insight into impermanence, or the passing nature of suffering, we do not become apathetic, feeling that nothing matters. We recognize suffering as suffering, and we allow that recognition to give rise to an aspiration to gain liberation from it. This is not apathetic. But we also realize that it is fruitless to get into a turmoil or become anxious about our suffering. We can abandon the habit of becoming anxious about suffering and simply recognize it and allow that recognition to give rise to a desire for liberation.

2

Working with Those Who Suffer

Stephen Levine: Your Holiness, in some environments the suffering is so intense that even though, as Joanna Macy says, we've built incredible mechanisms of denial, "reality" nonetheless breaks through and we cannot elude the pain.

When my wife and I were working with dying children, we sat next to the bed of a thirteen-year-old girl who was dying of leukemia, and her hair and eyes reminded us very much of our daughter. She pulled on our places of attachment and fear. How, in the face of such attachment and suffering, can we maintain compassion so that fear does not limit our ability to serve?

Dalai Lama: If, in order to lessen a person's suffering, you yourself share some of the suffering, that can help the other person. You relieve some of the burden. When I hear someone complaining about some unfortunate things, I join with him or her and mention, "You are not alone. Many people, including myself, feel the same." It is a matter of practice. There are many examples in Buddhism of highly-realized bodhisattvas, who are able to see and feel another person's suffering even more clearly than the person himself. Geshe Langri Thangpa, for example, had such deep insight into the nature of suffering that it is said that he only laughed three times in his entire life.

Stephen Levine: What did he laugh at?

Dalai Lama: I can't remember. One had to do with mice. He was called Langri the Weeper because he wept so much.

If you go more deeply into your own spiritual practice, emphasizing wisdom and compassion, you will encounter the suffering of other sentient beings again and again, and you will have the capacity to acknowledge it, respond to it, and feel deep compassion rather than apathy or impotence. When contemplating suffering, do not fall into depression. When reflecting on happiness, do not fall into the feeling of self-importance or conceit. Cultivating wisdom helps us avoid these pitfalls. But it is hard to generalize because each person's courage and forbearance are unique. These are the characteristics that enable us to acknowledge and respond to the suffering of others.

Stephen Levine: We use the term "burnout" to mean a profound fatigue from confronting so much suffering, a sense of helplessness and even hopelessness in the face of our inability to take away another's suffering. It seems that burnout is a resistance to suffering. How can we open ourselves to suffering in a way that allows it to come in? When I was working with dying children, if they were in a lot of pain, I would sit next to their bed and pray that something would alleviate their enormous suffering. That went on for years, until one day something inside of me said that that prayer was inappropriate. The most you can hope is that they get as much out of this as possible, that something in them will allow growth and healing from this. How do we allow ourselves to be in the face of suffering without resisting the suffering?

Dalai Lama: Meditation practice is also like that. If you try very hard, agitation, tightness, lethargy, or dullness will enter your mind. The more you struggle, the more your mind will become exhausted. The best thing you can do at such a point is to leave the meditation and refresh yourself. It is not effective to continue under that circumstance.

In dealing with those who are undergoing great suffering, if you feel "burnout" setting in, if you feel demoralized and exhausted, it is best, for the sake of everyone, to withdraw and restore yourself. The point is to have a long-term perspective. If, for the time being, you have to withdraw from active service, keep a long-term attitude in mind, so that you can continue to serve over the long term.

Jean Shinoda Bolen: Your Holiness, I was a bit worried when you mentioned the fellow who laughed only three times in his life, until I heard that he was called "The Weeper," because it sounds as if he was a man who was not afraid to break down and cry in the face of suffering. Often, as professionals and as adults, especially men, we are afraid of showing emotions and crying. Truly, if you are moved by the suffering of another person, that suffering may get through to you, and you may weep.

I want to ask you about showing feelings, about weeping, about being moved by your heart. It is my impression that people who meditate very often withdraw from suffering instead of going into it and sharing their very heartful reaction with the person in pain. Would you encourage people to show their feelings? Have you yourself ever been moved to weep in the presence of suffering?

Dalai Lama: As I mentioned earlier, there are two basic responses to suffering: one is to ignore it and the other is to look right at it and penetrate it. The appropriate response, for a meditator or anyone else, is to go into it, not simply to avoid it.

The same is true of one's own feelings. Whether they are pleasurable or unpleasurable, the point is to be aware of them. And to express them, yes. Talking about my own behavior, of course there are occasions when I weep in public.

Jean Shinoda Bolen: It is wonderful that you both laugh and weep in public. You are a remarkable role model for leaders.

Stephen Levine: Your Holiness, I completely agree with what Jean said, but I want to ask this about the weeping lama: does his weeping signify attachment?

Dalai Lama: There are two kinds of love and compassion. There is true compassion, also called love with reason, and there is the usual kind of love, which is very much involved in desire and attachment. Love or compassion based on attachment is limited and unstable. It is mainly a projection.

For example, someone very beautiful appears, and you want him or her to become yours. That kind of love is based on illusion. As soon as the situation changes slightly, the attitude changes also. Today you are in love, but tomorrow you may feel hostile. Isn't that true? With true compassion, you can see the other person's suffering, and your love develops from that. With this kind of love, as long as the other person is suffering, you can face it. That is not a projection.

Love based on attachment is not at all helpful. It just brings us irritation. But love based on reason is something that we need. With this kind of love, whether you say "my friend" or "my enemy," there is no difference. Your enemy suffers, and your friend also suffers. Since both are suffering, it is the same. This is the key: whether a person is your enemy or your friend, it doesn't matter.

Audience Question: How can we be comfortable with our shortcomings and our failings? When we see that we have been motivated by deluded parts of ourselves, how can we integrate this dark side?

Dalai Lama: The Buddhist approach is, first of all, to reflect on our faults and then to reflect on the long-term, destructive consequences of them. In Buddhism, there is a lot of emphasis on meditating on the truth of suffering. This may be a bit depressing, but when we see our faults clearly, we also see the possibility of freeing ourselves from them. Seeing our faults has very much to do with our capacity for awakening.

From a Buddhist point of view, no error is impossible to be changed. There is always a possibility for change. The recognition of our human intelligence can help us have more confidence in facing difficult situations. This is very important. When you feel discouraged, "I'm too old," "I'm not intelligent enough," "I've done too many evil things in the past," or "I'm simply not good enough," a common Buddhist practice is to study the lives of past generations of Buddhist adepts who acted even worse than you did or were even more foolish. Doing this, you will see that they were able to attain liberation, and you will realize, "If they could do it, I can do it too." You see your situation in a relative context, not just in the extreme, such as "I am simply too old."

I would like to invite you to respond to this question also. What are your reflections on this?

Stephen Levine: In our experience, if we're working with someone who has a profound pain, maybe from the loss of a loved one or a situation in their lives that seems unworkable, we find that if someone else who has also had this same pain works with them, that person's openness and compassion helps the situation very much. There is great compassion and a deep sense of our own inner power when someone who has been abused and worked through the pain serves others who are abused.

Those who have had children die, when they have allowed the pain in, can help others in the same situation. They have room in their heart for their pain so they have room in their heart for another's pain as well, and the healing power of their empathy and compassion is a little like priming a pump. They put a little bit of compassion in, and then one's own natural compassion and goodness arises. We get a lot of confidence when we experience our own natural goodness, even if we see that there are times we are not completely honest, or frightened, or feel very separate from ourselves and even the thing we love most. But when we are serving others, a confidence arises that even accepts how incomplete we are, and we become very whole, in a very heartful way.

Your Holiness, this touches a point that I think is very important. When people who feel themselves unloved fall into depression because of having been abused or for whatever reason, compassion itself helps them overcome or rise from the depression. Often when people are depressed, it is a good sign. It means they have found that the old ways don't work, and they're right! The old ways don't work. When the ways of self gratification, of "I" and "other," no longer make them happy, there is a possibility of discovering real happiness. So when I see people who are depressed, it doesn't depress me.

Dalai Lama: Yes, yes. True. Beautiful.

Audience Question: There is a great deal of concern nowadays about addictions of various kinds—to drugs, power, sensations, or even security. What specific methods or technologies can you suggest for people to deal with those attachments and addictions?

Dalai Lama: In Buddhism, we do not generalize about these matters. We always address ourselves to the individual who is having the difficulty, and then we apply specific treatment for that individual. As this is important for spiritual practice, I suspect it would be applicable for cases of addiction.

Daniel Goleman: This brings up another topic that we wanted to raise with Your Holiness, and that has to do with facing or not facing suffering, when you yourself are the one who is committing the act that creates the suffering. It is a question about the danger of detachment, in terms of not taking responsibility for the consequences of one's own act.

Joel Edelman: I wanted to share some experiences I had in the early and mid-1960s. I was in Vietnam with Daniel Ellsberg in 1963, working for the Rand Corporation—researching, advising, studying, and flying all over the country, helping choose targets. I flew twenty-five combat missions in which bombs were dropped or targets chosen. During that time, I had no awareness of anger or fear in myself, or even of the suffering that was being brought about by the bombing.

After nine months there, I had nothing more to do with military work. But on some level, I knew that I had done something wrong, and it was terribly difficult to deal with that. So I tried to suppress it, and I did not deal with it for many years. I refused to see any movies about Vietnam or read any books about it, and I didn't talk much about it either. It was just too much.

Finally, some years later, I was able to begin dealing with it in an indirect way by doing some good work. I had gone to law school, and I started to help relieve the suffering of some people who were poor and disadvantaged. Slowly I began to be able to talk about Vietnam. Then I began some psychotherapy to get in touch with what must have been a lot of anger and pain, and later I began Buddhist practice.

With this combination of Western psychotherapy and Eastern spiritual practice, a lot of suppressed pain started to surface. This psychic numbing is similar to the experience of many Vietnam veterans. More than 100,000 of them are said to have died violently, the majority by committing suicide. That means that more American veterans killed themselves since returning than were killed in Vietnam.

Dalai Lama: If one can generalize, what is the chief cause for all of these suicides? Is it guilt?

Daniel Brown: There are a number of contributing factors. One is that many people who go to the battlefield—in any war, including Vietnam—find that when they are in active fighting, they are given permission to kill, and that somehow changes them. They become different, biologically; they get more "excitement." In long-term therapy, veterans, at some point in the therapy, will tell you of the thrill, the excitement of killing. They often find it to be a physiological high. When they return to society, they put the aggression and the intense excitement out of their awareness. It is not acceptable to them or to society.

When soldiers return after most wars, there are culturally defined ways to help them take a different perspective. In this society, a parade is held and soldiers are told that they were heroes, having killed for a good cause. But in a war like Vietnam that was unacceptable to so many American people, there was no socially defined way to help the soldiers come to accept what was done. So the veterans were left to handle their feelings individually, rather than through societal rituals to help them transform that aggression into something more acceptable and to settle with it.

These veterans are very lonely. They have intense hatred as well as intense guilt, and they put both out of their awareness. On occasion, their consciousness changes; they go into "dissociative states," where the aggression comes up strongly, and they can either act it out on themselves (hurt or kill themselves) or on someone else (hurt or kill someone else).

What is striking to us about studies of war veterans is that when people are given permission to kill others, or even if they are the victims of extreme abuse like child abuse or torture, they seem to change biologically, psychologically (in terms of their ordinary sense of self), and also interpersonally, in terms of their understanding of the rules of social behavior. After that, anything goes. They are like different people. Working with this magnitude or quality of hatred is different from the kind of hatred we have been talking about. It is much more difficult to work with in therapy.

Margaret Brenman-Gibson: The distance from the target also makes a difference. In World War II, for instance, those who gave the orders way behind the lines, without witnessing the atrocities, or picking up the pieces, found it far easier to do their jobs and not have the kinds of conflict afterwards that these other people do.

Dalai Lama: But wasn't there comparable aggression and violence in terms of actual hand-to-hand combat and so forth, in the Second World War? What number of suicides were there among those veterans when they returned?

Daniel Goleman: Many fewer. When they came back, everyone said, "That was a good cause, you're a hero." Vietnam was considered a bad cause.

Dalai Lama: Since in both of these cases, during the action on the battlefield there was a lot of excitement and violence, it was not the initial aggression that was the cause for the suicide. It was society's response to the soldiers when they returned home. When the soldiers found that their actions appeared to be fruitless and wrong, they felt some kind of regret or self-contempt. So it seems to be a mixture of guilt and also a fresh hostility and aggression. Not simply the one from the war, but a new one created in the social context.

Joel Edelman: I felt a great deal of excitement when I was in Vietnam, and the excitement was a cover-up for much of what was going on underneath. There were no feelings of overt aggression associated with it, no feelings at all, but later the guilt really came out. I can identify with the feeling of wanting to self-destruct out of that guilt, of wanting to commit suicide.

Dalai Lama: Have you found any difference between those who engage in direct contact, that is, those who have someone in the sights of their gun, and those who are behind the scenes, behind the lines, giving the orders? Both are killing, but one is direct and the other is indirect.

Daniel Brown: In the research, the difference between being behind the lines or in direct combat was not the main variable. The main difference seemed to be exposure to atrocity. For example, sometimes people would watch other people get killed, like women and children. Sometimes people would watch other people get tortured. Sometimes the medical staff would go up after a battle and have to pick up the parts of the bodies. These people had as much difficulty, and sometimes more difficulty, than the people who were actively fighting.

Dalai Lama: Those who were engaging in the aggression were doing it, in a sense, voluntarily, while these other ones were just witnesses, in a more passive way.

Daniel Brown: The people who were more passive had more psychological difficulties. That is, of all of the groups, the people who have had the most psychological difficulties were the medical 'vacs, that is, the people who had to go and pick up the pieces of the bodies after a battle. The people who were engaging in aggression had less psychological difficulty.

Dalai Lama: This is really a tragedy. We can sympathize with these people; they were in an unbearable situation. It may be less unbearable if you are actually engaging in the aggression. This is very understandable because the ones who are actually engaging in the aggression have agreed somehow to do this, whereas the other people did not make that agreement. They are really victims.

Daniel Brown: Researchers found that if they gave guns to the people who were working with evacuating the wounded and the dead, even though they never used them, if they had the idea that they could use them and become active, they did not suffer the same kind of psychological damage as the people who didn't have guns.

Dalai Lama: Was there any difference between men and women in the medical staff?

Daniel Brown: I don't know.

Dalai Lama: Among these Vietnam veterans that you have treated who are suffering from intense guilt, hatred, anger, and aggression, what do you find is the most effective advice or guidance that you can offer them? What kind of counseling proves to be most effective—sympathizing with the hardships that they underwent in the war or disapproving of it and coming to terms with that?

Daniel Brown: Since a great deal of the pain and suffering has to do with the loneliness, guilt, and intense aggression that gets stimulated in that kind of war, as well as the helplessness and hatred that occurs when getting rejected by society after the war, the single best treatment has been group therapy, where people who have gone through the same kinds of experiences can talk openly about them, without blame or shame. It undercuts their isolation.

Dalai Lama: As part of your counseling, do you offer them the approval that they have not received from society?

Daniel Brown: In a group, at least they find a resolution of the shame and the blame, and get some acceptance, at least among the group members. From that, they often begin to make new meaning of their experience.

Jean Shinoda Bolen: If you have killed, if you have done things that make you feel unacceptable, and then your countrymen treat you as if you are unacceptable, the one thing that brings you back into humanity is another human being listening to your story, loving you, being compassionate for what you have gone through. Very often, what made the difference for Vietnam veterans was that another human being listened and listened to the bad dreams, to the dreadful things that the person had done, and somehow one other human being's compassion made it possible for that veteran to be part of humanity again. Sometimes that took place in therapy, but it also clearly took place between human beings who cared about one another. If there is one thing that has helped heal Vietnam veterans, it is compassion.

Dalai Lama: I would like to ask this question: How do psychotherapists help people with hallucinations or fantasies—people who are suffering with schizophrenia? From what I know, it is often emphasized that if you don't have a solid sense of ego or self, then you are bound to have personality conflicts, such as conflicts of identity, and so on. Is solidifying the ego the basis on which you work to help these patients?

Jean Shinoda Bolen: The first basis is having a relationship with your patient. The psychotherapist must begin with love and compassion. He or she must accept and connect emotionally with the patient who is suffering with schizophrenia, so that there is some human, heartful connection with that person. That helps stabilize the mind and heart of the patient.

We also have many useful medications, called "major tranquilizers," that serve as what we might call "ego glue." That is, they help the patient have a sense of an observing mind, and it helps them to know what to pay attention to. You see, the schizophrenic doesn't know what to pay attention to. He or she is tuning in or listening in or paying attention to too many fragmentary things. The medications reduce or eliminate the hallucinations so that the person is able to be in the world. It is difficult to be in the world if you are hearing voices that other people don't hear. You need to connect with other people in the world, and usually that comes through a relationship with your therapist. This is one way of describing how psychotherapists take care of schizophrenic patients.

The other way is to help the patient make sense of the experience he or she is having. People, when they are schizophrenic, sometimes move into that realm of what would be called the symbolic unconscious, like the images of all the deities on the Kalachakra wheel. A schizophrenic may be plunged into that world of light forms and demonic forms and lose himself in it. So the therapist can try to help make meaning of the experience.

Daniel Brown: As clinicians, we have also been struggling with how to develop good methods to treat people who have experienced extreme abuse or torture, and we have found that people go through various stages of recovery, and at each stage there are certain methods that are useful. In your experience, and particularly your experience with your people, many of whom have also undergone this extreme kind of abuse and torture, what do you find helps people overcome the kind of harm that has been done to them?

Dalai Lama: In the case of Tibetans, usually I tell them that this tragedy is very sad, very unfortunate. This is the darkest period in all of Tibetan history. But one way we can perceive such a tragedy is to see it as a good opportunity to test our integrity, our inner strength. Then, instead of being overwhelmed, we can increase our determination and strength.

Sometimes people misunderstand the theory that things happen, generally speaking, due to past karma. Obviously, these things happen due to social injustice. Here, you see, we must distinguish between two levels; otherwise, it is easy to misunderstand the Buddhist notion of karma. We need to understand what is the primary cause and what are the contributing circumstances. In the case of great suffering coming about as a result of social injustice, we can say that the primary cause behind it is the karma of the individuals involved. The contributing conditions that allow that karma to ripen are the social injustices that are evident. So, for example, in the case of the Tibetans, the suffering the Tibetans actually experience arises essentially from their own karma; that is the primary cause, their own actions in previous lives. But the condition that allows that karma to ripen is the Chinese oppression. And so, to fight against conditions of social injustice is most appropriate.

Daniel Goleman: Your Holiness, one question that arises is whether the experience of deep suffering can be used to help someone change, to become more compassionate. What is your view on whether going through deep suffering can in some cases be beneficial?

Dalai Lama: Yes, this certainly does happen. It is in the nature of suffering. In the case of suffering, regardless of the causes, however it might arise, once the suffering has been experienced, then if it is joined with certain types of influences, it may lead to depression, even long-term depression. But if it is joined with other circumstances, more skillful in means, then it can lend itself to greater courage.

Daniel Goleman: What are those elements that lead to greater courage?

Dalai Lama: First you must examine whether it is possible to overcome the problem. If there is a way out, then there is no need to worry. If there is no way out, then there is no point to be depressed. The reason we feel mental anguish is that we do not desire suffering or pain. But if we become obsessed with our suffering and become depressed and overwhelmed by it, that will further increase the suffering. If the suffering has already occurred, it is best simply to leave it. Then it will not have anything added on to it. Don't compound what has happened in the past by pondering it and accentuating it. Simply leave the past to its own devices and carry on in the present, taking steps to avoid such suffering in the present and the future.

3

Dealing with Anger

Audience Question: Sometimes I have to work with people who really annoy me. How can I accept them and use the opportunity for personal growth?

Dalai Lama: You must deal with each individual case. Look at one person who annoys you, and, if you can apply your practice to him or her, use the opportunity to counter your own anger and cultivate compassion. But if the annoyance is too powerful—if you find the person so repulsive that you cannot bear to be in his or her presence—it may be better to look for the exit! Here is the principle: it is better not to avoid events or persons who annoy you, who give rise to anger, if your anger is not too strong. But if the encounter is not possible, work on yourself by yourself. In the context of Buddhism, with regards to mental distortions, especially hostility and anger, it is standard practice to reflect again and again on their disadvantages and destructive nature, and by doing so, the mental affliction will gradually diminish.

I understand that in Western psychotherapy, repressing these mental afflictions is said to have very bad effects on both the body and the mind. I have heard that some people say, "You must express hostility when it arises." Are there any practices in Western psychotherapy, not simply for avoiding the repression, but for actually reflecting on the disadvantage of anger? Not just when it arises, but generally to reflect on the disadvantages of anger and thereby to dissipate it. Generally speaking, do you feel that it is better to feel repeated anger towards another person, or is it better not to? If you really feel that it is better not to feel anger, then wouldn't it be advantageous to find methods that prevent its arising in the first place? If you feel that it is better to decrease anger, does it help in the decreasing of anger to express it when it arises or not to express it?

Daniel Goleman: Your Holiness, there is no one answer. There are more than two hundred different schools of psychotherapy, and each has its own answer to your question, ranging from full expression to non-expression.

There is a body of evidence that comes from research, not from clinical practice, that shows that people who express their anger openly simply learn to express their anger openly. That is to say, the more you do it, the more easily it comes. That is a fact, a given. Another body of research shows that the more readily you express anger, the more prone to every kind of disease you are—heart disease, cancer, colds. These are two arguments for not expressing anger. However, within psychotherapy, there are many points of view.

Jean Shinoda Bolen: My experience is specific to the persons I have worked with. There is a first principle of knowing what it is you feel. Too often, with certain kinds of families, children learn to suppress their feelings, and they grow up numb, not knowing what they feel. It is important to find out the feelings and actually be able to tap them and express them.

There is an effort to develop an observing ego, or an observing mind, that then understands when the emotion comes up and what sets it off. Often, it is fear, a repetition of something that was hurtful in the past. Those kinds of insights help the person move away from the situation. Also, we often find that people are angry at someone because he or she resembles a significant negative figure in our past. We call this "transference."

Daniel Goleman: To give an example, Your Holiness, if your parent beat you as a child, and then later in life you have someone who resembles in some way the parent, you may feel anger toward this person. They may not have done anything to you, but you feel the anger from childhood toward that person. That is what is called transference.

Jean Shinoda Bolen: A person often needs to learn that the anger that he or she has been bottling up for so long will not destroy the therapist or make them a regrettable person if they express it. That is a learning process.

Often what we do in therapy is to "re-parent" a very damaged child who is still in the adult. But we are not helping that person learn to express anger easily or just spread the anger around. We are talking about a very unhappy person, in which something is not right. He or she should be combining the work of a spiritual practice with psychological practice. In my own Jungian analytic work, the two are not separated. A spiritual element is assumed to be an essential part of the human being, in the blood, so to speak, and it needs to be tapped.

Daniel Goleman: To summarize, if I may, the person will then feel the anger that comes from childhood toward the therapist, and the therapist will encourage them to express the anger verbally and, at the same time, to observe it with observing mind.

Dalai Lama: Are you saying that if you are not able to learn how to express your emotions as a child, they bottle up in yourself and you don't develop your personality fully? Therefore, it is better to express them so that you can identify and observe the different states of emotions and learn to respond to situations that might give rise to them. Is that what you are saying?

Jean Shinoda Bolen: Yes.

Dalai Lama: I feel that there might be a difference between the mental conflicts that one feels and the emotions they give rise to—anger, hostility, and so forth. If you are not able to express the mental conflicts that you have, then at a later point of your life, when you are able to express these mental conflicts, they are automatically accompanied by hostility and anger. Therefore it is important to express the suffering, not so much the hostility, but rather the suffering.

Jean Shinoda Bolen: Exactly. That is also the point in therapy. Anger and hostility are often the first layer. The suffering is underneath them.

There is also a difference between anger and hostility. We see anger in children when they are frustrated, when they cannot get their way, when they have tried to do something and it hasn't worked. There are lots of reasons for getting angry based on frustration, and yet children are not hostile unless they have been maltreated.

Dalai Lama: I would like to return to this question: Leaving aside one's whole history and childhood experiences, if one meets with something unpleasant right now and one feels anger, is it best to express it or not to express it, if one's basic wish is to decrease anger, to be free of it?

Daniel Brown: Sometimes in analytic therapies, such as psychoanalysis, people emphasize working with the negative mind states. After many years, certain patients would complete their therapies. They would not have any symptoms of depression. For example, they would have some insight into negative mind states, like anger. But they would not be nice people. So we have learned from such unfavorable outcomes of therapy that an emphasis on positive qualities is also necessary, but we have not developed that emphasis on cultivating positive mind states as much in our therapies as Buddhism has.

Dalai Lama: It is like simply being aware of the first two noble truths, suffering and the source of suffering, and never getting around to the third and fourth truths of liberation and the path to liberation.

Stephen Levine: I think a lot of us are trying to discover a middle way between the expression of anger and non-injury. We know that we cannot let go of anything that we don't accept, so we need to make room in our heart for even anger and those states of mind that are so hidden and subtle that not much awareness reaches them. These states, so associated with confusion and injury in the past, need to be given space if we are to have access to them now. Gone uninvestigated, these states sometimes surprise us when we are under stress.

We are trying to discover how to allow this quality of anger not to be suppressed or repressed, but to come fully into our awareness, so that it can be met and investigated, and seen as empty and changing. It seems that if we don't allow it to come up, we cannot investigate it.

Dalai Lama: But as it comes into the mind, should it also come out of the mouth?

Stephen Levine: If it comes into the mind wholeheartedly, there is no compulsion to act on it. It can float in space.

Daniel Brown: In psychotherapy the person may be encouraged to use fantasy to imagine all of the possible ways of expressing his anger and all of the consequences of expressing it. In that way, the person is not directing the anger in a destructive way toward the therapist or toward someone else. He or she is using fantasy as a way of imagining and shaping possibilities of expression.

Often, when people allow themselves to express their anger in fantasy and to verbalize those fantasies in therapy, some insight occurs. They may, for example, understand that the anger really isn't about the therapist or this other person, but is conditioned by some event in their past. They may discover that the anger is not the real feeling, but that they are feeling hurt or betrayed or rejected.

At that point, there's a space that one finds, where the anger can be there in awareness, without the need to do anything with it. And that awareness without the need to act is a kind of middle path between the extremes of having it hidden from awareness (suppressing it) or the compulsion to act upon it in a destructive way.

Dalai Lama: That's excellent.

Margaret Brenman-Gibson: Perhaps the question is not to find a middle ground or a moderate ground, but rather, to explore the possibility of integrating the dark side, or the aversive emotions, with the positive side. The great revolution that Erik Erikson brought to psychotherapy was to say that what we are trying to do, from the beginning of our development as babies, is "mutuality." For instance, in a transaction between a nursing mother and a baby, both people are getting something positive. It is not a question of one person simply giving and the other simply taking; it is a mutuality. That is a good model for psychotherapy and also for human development.

The real aim, then, is for an integrated ground, so that that part of the self, instead of going to war with another part of the self—judging and being punitive—will be compassionate to the other part of the self. We would call that a "benevolent superego." Or more simply: the path to self-forgiveness may be to find a new channel, a new mode of expression for our destructive, hateful impulses. It is necessary to find an integrating way for someone arguing within himself, a husband who is arguing with his wife or two nations in conflict. The aim is always the same—to find a creative, negotiated solution, whether it is inside yourself, between two people, or between two nations.

Daniel Brown: Many of the Buddhist writings on the practice of patience seem to assume that the practitioner is aware of his anger and can then find a way of practicing with it. In Western psychotherapy, many of the writings make a very different assumption—that the people who come for treatment are not aware of their anger. In fact, they have psychological defenses to keep it out of their awareness.

The Buddhist texts tell us a lot about how people who are aware of their anger can practice with that anger, but they tell us less about how to work with people who are not aware of their anger. Western psychotherapy tells us a lot more about how to work with people like the bomb-makers, who have no idea that their very profession has a lot to do with aggression, and who do not see it as aggression and do not experience the anger.

Dalai Lama: This is something that we as Buddhists need to learn about. This subconscious anger, if it has a parallel in Buddhist writings, would have more to do with what is called mental unhappiness or dissatisfaction, in the sense that this is regarded as the source for anger and hostility. We can see it in terms of a lack of awareness, as well as an active misconstruing of reality.

Margaret Brenman-Gibson: Dan Goleman has written a book about self-deception; sometimes we don't even know that we are angry in the first place. The kind of self-deception that involves a denial of what is happening emotionally inside of us, is very dangerous in the long run.

For example, I have been studying the people who make nuclear bombs. It is my impression that, by and large, these people do not feel angry at the world or even at the Russians. They do not feel that they are preparing for the possibility of destroying the world. They certainly have no intention to destroy the world. There is a tremendous denial and self-deception in these men and women.

Daniel Goleman: The problem is this, Your Holiness: many times people will engage in an action like making atom bombs and not realize the consequence of what they are doing. That is, they fool themselves. How can one deal with that? It is a big problem in therapy. Many people who come to psychotherapy do not even realize what their problem is. It is true of alcoholics, for instance. How can you help someone see through their own self-deception?

Dalai Lama: In the case of making bombs, the people involved are specialists, and they are focusing on something very narrow and becoming extremely expert in that area, without seeing the broader consequences of their acts. It is a kind of tunnel-vision. As long as they focus on that, the self-deception is supported. From the exploitist's viewpoint, this is a great achievement. In their own right, in their own domain, they are doing something extraordinary.

Margaret Brenman-Gibson: "Highly creative," one of them told me. People ask, "How can you be studying the creative process in bomb-makers? You must be crazy." I say, "No. In this narrow area of expertise, they are doing something creative." It is about the uses of their creativity that they are deceiving themselves.

Dalai Lama: This can also happen in the domain of spirituality or religious practice. One can focus very narrowly on one's own religious denomination or practice and become a fanatic in the process.

Daniel Goleman: Is there any solution to that problem?

Dalai Lama: Education.

Daniel Goleman: We need a wider context.

Stephen Levine: Your Holiness, in the case of the Vietnam War, the problem for those 100,000 men and women veterans who have committed suicide since the end of the war was not just the hostility of war, but the hostility of peace. These people who were marching with signs that said "PEACE" were spitting on these soldiers and calling them baby-killers as they got off the airplanes. These soldiers were seventeen-, eighteen-, and nineteen-year-old Blacks, Hispanics, and poor whites, the disenfranchised, the least powerful in our society. This exemplifies the issue of unexplored anger—people making war in the name of peace.

The protestors were judging these psychically wounded men and women, who were coming back, and cursing them. It wasn't just that their service was not accepted. Their desperate bravery was actually rejected. It was more than an absence of what the soldiers received when they came home from the Second World War. It was exactly the opposite. They got judgment, hatred, and rejection, and were called murderers by those who marched for peace with hostility in their hearts. If our anger is not explored, how do we really make peace?

Dalai Lama: This is a theme I often emphasize—to bring forth world peace, we must have mental peace.

Joel Edelman: One week after coming home from Vietnam, I was in New York City, and I happened to be a bystander at an anti-war parade down Fifth Avenue. I was standing near some people who were against the marchers, and a fight broke out. Somebody who was carrying a sign that said, "PEACE NOW," hit me over the head with it. I got the point.

Margaret Brenman-Gibson: We must remember that some of the protestors were choosing the wrong place to put their terrible grief and rage at that wrongful war. If, indeed, they had had the truth of where the problem lay—namely, with the decision-makers who were sending these boys to kill, they would have known not to "kill the killer," but to pressure Congress to cut off the funds for the war. When they finally did that, it was a turning point in the whole situation. The people fighting the war were the wrong target.

Audience Question: Is it possible to transform the energy of anger? What can we do with the anger when we find ourselves in it? What specific practices do you propose?

Dalai Lama: It depends on how forceful the anger is. If it is not very forceful, you can try to look at a different aspect of the person. Every person, no matter how negative he or she seems to be, also has positive attributes. If you try to look at that side of them, the anger will immediately be reduced. This is one way. Another thing you can do is to try to find what is good or useful about the anger. If you try to find it, you'll see that you can't. Anger is really something awful. On the other hand, you can find many good things in patience, compassion, and love. Once you have that kind of genuine conviction, when anger begins to develop, you will remember its negativity and try to reduce it.

But when the anger is too forceful, you can try to direct your mind elsewhere, on some other thing. Just close your eyes and concentrate fully on your breathing. Count your breaths up to about twenty or twenty-five. Then the anger will be slightly reduced, slightly cooled down.

But if the anger is very, very strong, then fight! I am just making a joke. But really, it is better to express it than to hide it inside. A very negative, hateful feeling may remain there for years. That is the worst. Compared to that, it is better to say a few nasty words.

Stephen Levine: Your Holiness, does fear ever arise in your mind?

Dalai Lama: Oh, yes.

Stephen Levine: What do you meet that with?

Dalai Lama: I find that there are two types of fear. In one kind, things are quite delicate, or critical. At such times, I know that I must make a decision, whether I know what to do or not. First, I try to consult with my friends and reflect on it. Then, I make a decision and act, and I never feel regret. Ultimately, this is very much related to motivation. If I have no negative selfish motivation, deep down I will have no guilty feeling. When I act with sincere motivation, even if things do not go as expected, there is no regret.

A second kind of fear is based on imagination. To overcome that, you need calmness so that you can investigate it more closely. When you look into it in detail, your imaginary fear dissipates.

We have to look into individual cases. Sometimes, you see, there is real danger associated with some kinds of fear.

In that case, it is worthwhile to feel fear. Out of fear, you see how to take every proper precaution. It can be a serious loss if there is an actual danger and you feel no fear!

But another type of fear, when there is no imminent danger, is one you have created. With that kind of fear, the essential thing is to have sincere motivation and openness deep down. This is very helpful to reduce the fear. With self-confidence you can meet any person and talk with him or her. Even though you still have fear, because of your confidence, you have some kind of justice or truth within you. So, the basic things, I think, according to my own experience, are compassion and an altruistic mind.

4

Love and Compassion

Audience Question: Much of what we've talked about has to do with suffering and harmfulness. Can you say more about joy and happiness?

Dalai Lama: It is already happiness when someone decreases your suffering. We have a saying in Tibet, "If you are too excited by joy, later you will have to cry." This shows the relative nature of what we identify as joy and pain, and it implies that there should be a limit.

From a Buddhist practitioner's viewpoint, the important thing is that your mental state remain steady, not too many ups and downs. There are joys and pains, even depression, but not too low or too high. This way of life may seem colorless, but a more colorful, exciting way of life is, in a deep sense, not good. It is like having lighting in the room. If sometimes it is blindingly bright and other times it is too dark to see, it is not very useful.

This whole way of life depends mainly on mental attitudes, remaining calm and stable. This, I think, is most important. This stability of mind is developed through training. One's heart and mind become more resilient, firmer, less likely to be pushed around by external events. The opposite is too much sensitivity, so that the slightest negative input will agitate you or throw you into depression, and the slightest positive input will get you very excited. This is not helpful.

In the depths of your mind, you have wisdom that will carry you when you encounter something negative. You don't get thrown by it; you simply take it in stride. Likewise, when something good happens you can take this in stride, also. Taking things in stride is the key.

Daniel Brown: Your Holiness, I wish to ask a question about the inner nature of this practice. There seem to be two kinds of practices—those designed for working with the more negative, or non-virtuous, qualities of mind, and those that are designed to actively cultivate virtuous qualities. These seem to be complementary but independent practices. Working with negative states doesn't necessarily lead to the rising of positive qualities. One needs, in addition, to actively cultivate these virtuous qualities of mind like faith, patience, and an altruistic attitude.

In our society, a lot of the more analytically-oriented therapies, like psychoanalysis, have been emphasizing working with the negative qualities of mind. Other therapies, namely the transpersonal therapies, have said that isn't enough, that we also have to cultivate these positive qualities. So we are also struggling with the same kind of issues. How, in Buddhism, are these positive qualities developed?

Dalai Lama: To cultivate an altruistic attitude, a meditator takes the well-being of others to heart and reflects again and again on the benefits of caring for and cherishing them. But he balances this also by reflecting on the disadvantages of simply cherishing his own well-being, placing priority on himself as opposed to everyone else. These two facets of this meditation together lead to a wholesome state of mind.

Similarly, when he practices the cultivation of loving kindness, he balances this by countering hatred. These two also go together and are mutually helpful. Which should you emphasize in the beginning? We cannot make any uniform statement. It is really an individual matter.

Daniel Goleman: Your Holiness, we in the West have a model of mental health, of mental wholesomeness, that only goes part way. What is the Tibetan Buddhist model of mental health?

Dalai Lama: Ultimately, the only healthy person is a Buddha. But this is a bit far away. So, keeping our feet on the ground and looking at our present circumstance, we simply look to worldly convention to see when a person is healthy. When does society acknowledge a person as good or wholesome? There is nothing absolute here. One person might appear to be very fine, but then, when you see another person with even deeper compassion or greater wisdom, the first person appears to be inferior. There are no absolute criteria here.

But if you want to be more precise, you can say that a healthy person is someone who, when there is an opportunity to be of service to others, engages in that service. When that is not possible, he or she at least avoids causing harm. A person who does that is a healthy person. This is the essence of Buddhism. In fact, I believe that this is the essence of all spiritual traditions.

Daniel Goleman: So a single person loving someone who is unloved can open the way to compassion?

Dalai Lama: Yes, exactly.

Margaret Brenman-Gibson: That is very frequently the position in which a helper, a psychotherapist, finds him or herself—to be that one person who can genuinely feel love for this person who comes in suffering, in pain, and who has no sense of ever having found in him or herself anything lovable.

So I often say to students, after the first hour when they have seen somebody who is in great pain and who wants some help, "Do you like this person at all? Really, *honestly?*" And if the answer is, "I really don't," then I say, "Please let someone else be the therapist for this person. If you cannot see anything lovable in this person, that you can respond to in a genuine way, then you are not the right person to help this person."

Dalai Lama: Yes, absolutely. This is very true.

Daniel Goleman: It seems when people have been brought up feeling unloved or have been victimized, abused by parents, or so on, it is very hard for them to find compassion for other people. Your Holiness, how can you help someone who doesn't feel love for himself to be able to love others, to be compassionate?

Dalai Lama: If this person has never encountered love directed towards himself or herself from any quarter, if no one has ever shown this person love, it is very difficult. But if that person can meet even one person who will show unconditional love—simply acceptance and compassion— then even if he hasn't experienced compassion himself, if he knows that he is an object of someone else's affection and love, it is bound to have an impact, and this will be appreciated. Because there is a seed in himself, this act of love will start to catalyze or ripen that seed.

Stephen Levine: Your Holiness, I know many people who, after doing very profound work on themselves, come to a place where they find it difficult to experience joy in their lives. It is more than just the recognition of the suffering of grasping after satisfaction and pleasure. A profound sadness arises in many people I know who are of service to others. There is not a lot of joy in their lives. How can we learn to play in the Dharma?

Dalai Lama: Maybe you can extract a little bit from the Tibetan brain. Tibetans are really cheerful. I'm just kidding. When someone, through his whole life, experiences a lot of tragedies, it can be helpful to adopt the perspective that there are many past lives and future lives also. Then, even if one's present life appears hopeless, there is a broader context.

But I think you are not talking about a life filled with misfortune, but rather a life that is focused on spiritual practice and on serving, and, in the context of this, still feeling depressed and unhappy, not having the capacity for joy. In the process of meditation, one may gain a fairly deep insight into the nature of mind and the unsatisfactory nature of this cycle of existence. In the process, one develops a yearning to be free of this round of suffering. However, as a result of one's own personal practice and engagement with society, one may find that one's expectations were not fulfilled. You didn't do as well as you wanted, or expected to, and this disappointment can detract from your capacity for joy. So it may have something to do with expectations. One might have too many expectations in the beginning that can take away the joy later on.

Jean Shinoda Bolen: Your Holiness, I have a question about balancing detachment and compassion. In conventional Western psychotherapy, there seems to be a different level of closeness that we want to foster in a person—an ability to be closer to another human being than, I think, is encouraged and developed in Tibetan Buddhism. The Buddhist position, I think, is more like the position of the psychotherapist. As a psychotherapist, we have compassion and no judgment. We are detached; we observe the feelings in the other person and attempt not to get caught in our own feelings as we are in the process of doing our work. But if we were to go home with that kind of attitude, observe the people closest to us and not react to them, just watch them, think about them, and feel compassion towards them, then we aren't close enough to form an intimacy that will endure over the years and bring us into our own feelings.

One of the problems that psychotherapists have, that meditators may also have, is an inability after a while to react spontaneously to someone else's situation. Taking it further and further down the line, we could get to the detachment of the bomb-maker, where we are just too far away from the heart level, the reactive level, and the fear level—all the emotions.

There is a need to pull these opposites together—to be able to observe and be compassionate, and also to be intensely involved and care greatly, so that emotional loss will affect us, other people truly matter to us, and we will grieve deeply and be hurt deeply by them because they matter, not just because we have become pathologically detached or attached. There is a different optimal level, I think, that we foster in our work. I am raising this as an observation and also as a potential shadow side of meditation practice.

Dalai Lama: If one feels very profound compassion, this already implies an intimate connection with another person. It is said in Buddhist scriptures that we are to cultivate love just like that of a mother towards her only child. This is very intimate. The Buddhist notion of attachment is not what people in the West assume. We say that the love of a mother for her only child is free of attachment.

Jack Engler: Americans, in particular, often feel that we have a right to be happy. In fact, we get angry when we're not happy or when someone else gets something and we don't, or they get more of it. This seems to be built into many of the assumptions on which this country was founded.

It is different, I think, from the Buddhist notion that we can be happy. The idea that we have a right to it, and we have a right to it now, and we shouldn't have to wait for it, or we shouldn't have to work very hard to get it, is very destructive. But it is part of the American dream. Although the American Constitution says that we have a right to the pursuit of happiness, we usually think that means we have a right to have happiness all the time. This colors the way we act. If, for example, our Buddhist practice doesn't produce happiness immediately for us, we have little ability to assume the perspective of a bodhisattva and concentrate on service and compassion. Behind all of this tends to be the issue that our own happiness is paramount, and this is reinforced by our culture, over and over again.

Dalai Lama: It is natural to pursue one's own happiness and to work hard to get it now. But this is different from pursuing it while neglecting and ignoring, and even at the expense of, others' happiness. There is a big difference between the two.

Audience Question: Can you speak more about compassion in organizations—business organizations, social organizations, or government organizations? How can one help organizations act compassionately, as organizations?

Dalai Lama: On the one hand, there is no organization that is not composed of individuals. Apart from individuals, there are no organizations. So it is best to focus on the individuals in the organization, especially those who bear the most responsibility for it, and try to encourage in them a greater sense of awareness and compassion. If we can bring about a greater awareness of the benefits of compassion for society as a whole, this will be critical as a matter of survival.

Jean Shinoda Bolen: Can you say more on it being a matter of survival?

Dalai Lama: We have talked a lot about the crisis of contemporary civilization, the great turmoil, the problems we are encountering. What do these arise from? From the lack of loving kindness and compassion. If we focus on this, the benefits of compassion are obvious. Of course, the threat of nuclear weapons is extremely dangerous, but in order to stop this threat, ultimately the solution is compassion, realizing that other people are our human brothers and sisters.

Audience Question: I have noticed that children begin to lose compassion when they enter school and meet uncompassionate others. What suggestions do you have for children who must learn to handle people who do not have compassion, and still develop their own compassion?

Dalai Lama: It is very important that they have very close ties with their good friends, their wholesome friends, and with their parents, their own family. That is where the effort needs to lie, in very close and wholesome family ties. Apart from that, there is not much to do.

Human beings, when they are first born, start nursing on mother's milk. This is the first lesson in compassion and love. By nature, taking milk from our mother is, in itself, a lesson in human relations on the basis of affection. We must try to maintain that spirit. That is how we develop intimate relationships—based on affection between ourselves and our mother, through nursing on her milk. Compassion in the family is very important. If there is a compassionate atmosphere in the family, not only the parents but also the coming generations will benefit. Their mental and physical development will be much healthier.

I believe very deeply that compassion is the route not only for the evolution of the full human being, but also for the very survival of the human being, from conception through birth and growing up. To me, this is quite clear.

5

Buddhism in the West

Jack Engler: Your Holiness, when we Americans begin any endeavor, we start by asking questions. We tend to think in terms of finding a better technology. It is very important to us to begin any kind of a path with a Right View, so we have some context in which to understand what we are doing. When we come to the Buddhist tradition, we find that it begins with the peculiar story of the Buddha's great renunciation. A man, Siddhartha Gautama, abandons his family, his people, and his kingdom, and goes off on a personal, private search. But the story does not tell us much about what happens to his family or his people.

I am at a midpoint in my life, and I feel as if I have lived my life backwards. I started out as a practitioner of meditation and then, later on, I became a householder. Now I have a family, a home in the suburbs, two cars, and a job at which I work too many hours, and I am still on my search. I am very sincere about it, but I bring my family, my cars, and all these things along with me. I believe the Buddhist tradition suggests that one has to leave these things behind in order to follow the path. What does a monk like you, who has left those things behind, tell someone like me?

Dalai Lama: It is not at all the case that the path of the householder, fully engaged in society, is incompatible with the Buddhist path, despite the story of the Buddha's own life. It is possible to follow the path to liberation and Buddhahood as a householder. This is determined by your own interests and capacities, and also the needs of the society that you wish to serve.

I often advise people in the West who have newly and freshly entered the Buddhist path that it is important, as they pursue their spiritual practice, not to divorce themselves from Western society. Wherever you live, you must remain a good member of society. That is very important. In this society, where a monk is not a familiar role, if one were a Buddhist monk, it would be more difficult to integrate with the society, to interact with people in the society to bring any benefit. In this light, it may be better for a person to be a householder.

Daniel Brown: Your Holiness, in this culture, intimate relationships are also an important part of the path, of the search for truth. I have spent almost twenty years trying to meditate, sometimes intensely, in this country and in Asia. I have learned a little about the value of the continuity of awareness and also that if you spend many hours watching the states of mind arise, you can do it with less reactivity. Clinging and aversion still occur, but there is some distance from them. I also have found that if you watch that process of constant change in the mind, it is hard to find some solidity to the self. It is hard to see the ordinary self as self-existent. These have all been very useful lessons for me.

Like Jack, my path was backwards. Having practiced all that meditation, I then did a lot of psychotherapy, our

Western path, which meant five years of individual psychotherapy with a male therapist, and then nine years of
psychoanalysis with a woman. I found that doing therapy
and then psychoanalysis in this culture presented me with a
different sort of experience. There was something unique
about the quality of the relationship in therapy. In psychoanalysis, you lie on the couch and talk about your states of
mind four or five times a week for an hour. There is merit
and value in expressing such states of mind in the presence
of another person, whose explicit stance is not to be
reactive in the sense of blaming or criticizing you. You
learn about your own fear of being aware of and expressing
whatever comes into your mind, and you learn that you can
share those experiences without the fear of rejection or
blame. That was not something I had learned from meditation.

One of the things I wonder about is how to integrate
meditation and psychotherapy. I see them both as kinds of
awareness training, but one tells me more about insight
into the workings of the mind and the other tells me more
about intimacy, that is, how to be honest with myself with
another person. Both are useful, but I don't know how to
put them together. I wonder if Your Holiness would say
something about the nature of relationships and intimacy
as a path to practice, and also your impressions of Western
psychotherapy in this regard.

Dalai Lama: I don't have any experience in applying
Western psychotherapy to the Buddhist path. I do know,
however, that intimacy is necessary for a spiritual practitioner, especially if that individual is trying to overcome his
mental problems. When you open up yourself mentally, you

do so only with someone you trust from the bottom of your heart, someone you feel very close to. To open yourself up in this way is an important step in overcoming mental problems.

This is similar to the bodhisattva vow to dedicate your whole life to the benefit of others. You become something to be utilized by all sentient beings. "I am here for your use." If the other person understands that you are there simply for his well-being, it can be of great benefit. This is a basic Mahayana teaching dealing with the bodhisattva way of life.

This also relates to the question of attachment. As soon as we speak of intimate relationships, the question of attachment, or clinging is bound to come up. In the teachings of early Buddhism, it is said that clinging is the chief affliction of the mind, whereas in the later Mahayana teachings, hostility is regarded as the chief affliction of the mind. In the Mahayana teachings, attachment or clinging can be used on the path to help sentient beings.

Daniel Brown: I would like to pursue this a little further. If I am interested in using a relationship as a vehicle to pursue my practice and to pursue truth, I don't find any place in the Buddhist scriptures where this is clearly spelled out. For example, if I am having a fight with my wife, it may cause anger, pain, and aversion in me. At that point, it is useful for me to look at the state of my mind, and also to be somewhat self-transcending, to reach out and to say, "Maybe I wasn't sensitive or understanding enough," and I try to see her perspective. Then something in me shifts, we both realize some aspect of the truth, and the mental conflict, the afflictions, clear away.

I find those moments in my interaction with my wife and my friends to be very useful as vehicles for growth. But I do not see any way that this has been spelled out or clarified as to how one can do this as a practice in Buddhism. Is there such a vehicle?

Dalai Lama: Generally speaking, the teachings of the Buddha are designed to provide remedies for the distortions or afflictions of the mind, especially clinging and hostility. These can be applied whenever these afflictions

arise. If they arise in the context of an intimate relationship, such as in a conflict with your spouse, Buddhist
practice can definitely help. I think you already understand
that.

Daniel Brown: In the traditional accounts, practice usually
comes in stages. The Buddhist teachings on working
with afflictions can easily be applied to conflict with my
spouse. But what about insight? What about understanding
emptiness? What about stilling the mind? How can these
principles be applied in the context of an intimate relationship?

Dalai Lama: We can say that there are two domains of
spiritual practice. Some elements of spiritual practice are
more private, to be practiced alone for the cultivation of
insight. Other elements are better practiced in relationship
with others. In Buddhism, we engage with others chiefly to
be of service. These are two distinct realms, although they
are very much related.

It is easy to see how our practice can enhance our
relationship with others. It is also easy to see how our
interactions with others store merit, or spiritual potential,
in our own mind-stream, which then helps in our own
private practice. But the idea that our interactions with
others actually help our own insight is quite interesting. In
an intimate relationship, where love and attachment are
mixed, it is diffcult to say how this will help the individual
who is practicing. In a case where there is attachment or
clinging to another person, where the person is arising as a
very strong object and the attachment is arising with a

strong sense of "I"—"I love this person, I am grasping for this person"—if you see this as a false idea of self, you can have some insight into the notion of emptiness.

Daniel Brown: Can you please elaborate on that as a practice? How do you do that?

Dalai Lama: In that context, it is quite easy to see the absence of a self-sufficient, autonomous ego, or "self." So in times of very strong passion, whether hostility or craving, there arises a strong sense of self with the sense that the self, the "I," is substantial. We can feel the sense of ego, or self, at the moment it arises in the mind very distinctly and clearly. Then we investigate whether such a self exists in reality, and we find that it does not.

When the mind is not caught up by some affliction or distortion, the connection between the object and the mind that is perceiving the object is a continuous flow, and the momentary nature of perception may not be so evident. But when the mind is aroused by some passion, it becomes extremely agitated, and it is easier to realize the impermanence or transience of mental events. There is a lot of energy involved in the arising of hostility and attachment. Our task is not to fall into the pitfalls of these mental afflictions but to be able to use the energy that goes along with them.

Jack Engler: From a Buddhist point of view and also from a psychotherapeutic point of view, there seems to be an ideal that we should be above suffering and not be touched by it, that through equanimity, we can reach a stage where we are not affected by pain. I have the impression that this ideal is never helpful.

Stephen Levine: I'm not sure it is even possible not to be touched by another's pain when our hearts are engaged.

Jack Engler: Oh, it's possible. Therapists do it all the time.

Margaret Brenman-Gibson: Or they try to.

Stephen Levine: Not good therapists.

Margaret Brenman-Gibson: I am not in the least persuaded that it is useful for therapists to hold as an ideal the aim of "being above the suffering" of those who come for help.

Jack Engler: No, we do this all the time. Your Holiness, we have been talking a lot about the importance of a helping relationship in psychotherapy and spiritual practice. I remember hearing you say, "If you can't help, at least don't harm." You also said that if one is going to face one's suffering and penetrate it deeply, it needs to be done in the context of trust, safety, and understanding. That often means with another person or in a community, a sangha, with a teacher; and that brings the teacher and the student, or the therapist and the patient, into a very close, intimate relationship with each other. In some ways they even have to love each other. Maybe there is some combination of love and attachment, but the relationship is there and it grows.

That relationship poses certain vulnerabilities, dangers, and risks for both of them, particularly for the student or the patient. It is very sad that we see so much evidence of this today, where the helper has abused his or her position or power. In Boston, where I practice, almost every month the newspaper has headlines of another therapist who has been accused of misusing his or her power by his or her clients, usually men abusing women. We have also heard many similar examples in the Buddhist sanghas around the country of teachers who have abused positions of power and trust.

In my clinical practice, I am having more people come to me who have been abused by therapists. Recently, a number of therapists themselves have come who have abused their clients and are asking for help. It is very difficult to work with fellow therapists who have abused their clients, but we must. They need help as much as anyone else.

In Western psychotherapeutic training, one is taught how to anticipate these situations and deal with them in order not to fall into that danger. Even so, people fall. The risks are great. But at least the major professions that most therapists belong to—psychiatry, psychology, social work, nursing—are regulated by state licensing or certification boards that oversee professional conduct. Substantiated, ethical misconduct can lead to the therapist losing their license to practice in their profession. Clients also have recourse to civil or criminal action in the courts. Is there anything equivalent to this oversight function in Buddhism? How is that handled with Buddhist teachers? How is it handled in their training; and secondly, if it comes to public attention that some teacher is having difficulties in this area, how is that then handled in the teaching community?

Dalai Lama: Part of the blame lies with the students, because they pamper the spiritual teachers; they spoil them. In the Buddhist tradition, someone becomes a spiritual teacher in relation to a disciple. There isn't any particular license or piece of paper or degree that you give someone qualifying that person as a spiritual teacher. You are a lama because you have students.

In cultivating a relationship with a spiritual teacher it is important not to be too quick to consider that person to be your spiritual teacher, because it is a very powerful relationship. For however long it may take—two years, five years, ten years, or longer—you simply regard this other person as a spiritual friend, and, in the meantime, you observe closely that person's behavior, attitudes, and ways of teaching, until you are very confident of his or her integrity. Then there is no need for any license. But it is very important, from the beginning, to have a very firm, sound approach.

There isn't any aspect of the training towards becoming a lama that is specifically designed to help you avoid abusing your own students, if you ever have students. But the very nature of Buddhist practice is to cultivate compassion, a sense of altruism towards others, and if this is pure, then the teacher will not abuse his influence.

Jack Engler: That's a very big "if"—if one is pure enough. I think people enter into these relationships on the assumption that the teacher has some degree of enlightenment; and then, when the abuse takes place or similar mistakes are made, the disillusionment is quite strong.

Dalai Lama: I normally recommend to Buddhist practitioners not to see every action of their spiritual teacher as divine and noble. In all of the Buddhist teachings, there are specific, very demanding qualities that are required of a spiritual mentor.

If one has a teacher who is engaging in unsuitable or wrong behavior, it is appropriate for the students to criticize that behavior. It says very explicitly in the sutras, in the Buddha's own teachings, that in those aspects where the teacher's behavior is wholesome, you should follow in that teacher's footsteps, but where it is unwholesome, you should not. So when it is incompatible with the wholesome, when it is incompatible with the Buddhist teachings, then you don't follow in the guru's footsteps. You don't simply say, "It is good behavior because it is the guru's." This is never done. It states explicitly in the sutras that if the guru's behavior is improper, you should identify it as being improper and not follow it. It states explicitly that you should recognize the unwholesome as being unwholesome, so one might infer that it is worthwhile to criticize it. In one text of *The Highest Yoga Tantra,* it explicitly mentions that any advice that your teacher gives you that is unsuitable to your Buddhist way of life, your practice, should not be followed.

Jean Shinoda Bolen: But everything you've said puts the responsibility on the student, not on the one who is presumably more enlightened.

Dalai Lama: The guru, the spiritual teacher, is responsible for his or her improper behavior. It is the student's responsibility not to be drawn into it. The blame is on both. Partly it is because the student is too obedient and devoted to the spiritual master, a kind of blind acceptance of that person's guidance. That always spoils the person. But of course part of the blame lies on the spiritual master, because he lacks the integrity that is necessary to be immune to that kind of vulnerability.

Jack Engler: Your Holiness, the relationship of a student and a teacher starts as an unequal relationship, much as a therapeutic relationship does. One person has much more power and, supposedly, more wisdom, more insight. The other person is in the position of seeking help and is therefore much more vulnerable to being mistreated. I am concerned that the way you have presented this so far puts too much responsibility on the person who is being mistreated or victimized. It seems to me that the higher responsibility must reside, at least in the beginning, with the teacher or the therapist.

Dalai Lama: Yes, you are speaking quite practically. In fact it varies with different centers and different lamas. One thing that I have noticed is that most Dharma centers in the West have come into existence as a result of an individual teacher's contacts with a few students. These

Dharma centers did not come into existence as part of some program of a central organization, and, therefore, there has not been any way to check them. In the future, we are thinking about having some kind of central organization. I receive quite a number of letters complaining about these different teachers. Therefore, I think the time has come. We can do something.

The advantage of having this kind of central organization is that whenever a new Dharma center requires a teacher, a Board of Directors could recommend a particular teacher who possesses the basic qualifications that are necessary to be a spiritual teacher. Then, on the basis of such a recommendation, someone could be selected. When the selection has been made on the basis of an individual contact, it is often difficult for the student to have the knowledge to judge whether the spiritual teacher is suitable or not, qualified or not.

Imagine that a person has been appointed to be the head of a center and, after two or three years, this person's behavior starts to degenerate. At that time the Board could withdraw its support, saying, "You are no longer suitable."

Daniel Goleman: I think this is good news for many Dharma students—licensing for lamas. I think it is clear that the majority of teachers have been very good. It is a small group who have had problems, though you may know more than I do since you get so many letters.

Jack Engler: Your Holiness, in the relationship of students and teachers, where the teacher is abusing the student, dominating the student in an improper way because of the teacher's greater training, presumably greater wisdom, greater position of power, if this happens isn't it really the teacher who is guilty, rather than saying it's the student's fault because they were faithful too quickly? Do you feel that the responsibility really lies chiefly with the student?

Dalai Lama: No, in that case, the responsibility does lie chiefly with the teacher. When the person is supposed to be offering Dharma, offering spiritual teaching, and he himself indulges in an action that he has been preaching to others to avoid, then it's disgraceful. One can say that person has betrayed the task.

Margaret Brenman-Gibson: Your Holiness, I have a question concerning non-attachment. I hope I am not misquoting Joanna Macy to say that there is a common misunderstanding of the Buddhist teaching in that people, by way of seeking non-attachment, manage to divorce themselves entirely from the world. Isn't that a spiritual trap?

Dalai Lama: Within Buddhist practice, there are two kinds of attitudes towards attachment. It depends on your goal. If you are seeking individual liberation—for yourself alone— attachment is spoken of only as detrimental, something to be abandoned, avoided, and prevented. But if you are seeking liberation for the benefit of all living creatures and trying to be of service to all living beings, then there are cases where bodhisattvas are even encouraged to use attachment in their service for the benefit of others. There is a difference between the normal kind of attachment based on egotism and attachment based on a sense of intimacy with the living creatures you are serving. In the second case, attachment is not to be abandoned.

Is there some sense in Western psychotherapy that, up to a certain point, attachment is neutral or even beneficial, and only beyond that point does it become harmful? Is that kind of discrimination made?

Daniel Brown: I think there is a middle ground. Sometimes there is too much attachment, what we would call patho-logical attachment, and relationships become compulsive. There is too much desire. On the other hand, there are individuals who get too detached. They remain aloof, distant. They have some problem engaging in a relation-ship in an open and honest way with their feelings. Some-where in between is a kind of engagement that is healthy, and helping a client find that middle ground is useful.

Stephen Levine: Your Holiness, there may be some confu-sion in the West. I know when we read some Buddhist texts, there are descriptions of extraordinary events that beings go through on the way to self-knowledge. Some teachings seem to indicate that if you can't be abused and still stay compassionate, you'll never be a Buddha. There are stories of a monk walking down a road and robbers come upon him and saw off his arm, and, as he reaches the first stage of enlightenment, he sends mercy and compassion to his abusers. Then they saw off one of his legs and he reaches the second stage of enlightenment and sends loving kindness to them; and they take off his other arm, as his enlightenment deepens, his heart wide open, his mind perfectly clear. These kind of texts often leave one with a feeling of inadequacy and profound discouragement.

These can very easily be misinterpreted to mean, "If I cannot allow myself to be abused, I'm not a good Buddhist."

Dalai Lama: Do you mean if a spiritual teacher teaches you in a way that shows his cunningness and shrewdness because he is preparing a way to abuse you?

Stephen Levine: Very skillfully, too, I might add.

Dalai Lama: I think you should keep away from such teachers.

Audience Question: Your Holiness, can you give some guidance for beginning spiritual practice? How can we remain steady and simple in a complicated, materially-oriented society?

Dalai Lama: When you first start spiritual practice, you will probably do it with some intensity, a lot of momentum. At times during this stage, you might find it difficult to be simple and steady. But once you have some experience, it is not too difficult.

The environment where you begin your spiritual practice can make some difference. In America, there are many remote places. You can go to one of these places for a few weeks and do your practice intensely. But, as far as

Tibetan Buddhism is concerned, when you practice, you do not isolate yourself from the rest of the society. That is important. Sometimes I notice that certain individuals have a lot of enthusiasm for isolating themselves from the rest of society. In these cases, after a few years, there are usually some problems. Therefore, I think it is better to remain with a community.

I also think it is very important to remember that you are a Westerner. Your social and cultural background and your environment are different from mine. If you want to practice an Eastern philosophy, such as Tibetan Buddhism, you should take the essence and try to adapt it to your cultural background and the conditions here. As you engage in spiritual practice, for example, Buddhism, over the course of time, you can gradually integrate it with your own culture and the values here, just as in the past occurred with Indian Buddhism, Tibetan Buddhism, and so on. There must gradually evolve a Western Buddhism or an American Buddhism.

6

Making a Difference
through Compassionate Action

Jack Engler: Your Holiness, when I was young and full of
energy and idealism, I wanted to act compassionately in the
world, but I didn't know how to be effective, how to make a
difference. So I looked for ways to change myself, and I
found a tradition of Buddhist practice that focused on
going inside and investigating the self. But in my single-
minded pursuit of that, I often neglected family, friends,
work, society, and other responsibilities.

Now I'm old and gray! I've learned how to be more
effective in the world and devote a lot of time to service
both in my professional work and in other ways. But now I
find that I have the opposite problem—I often get so
caught up in the activities of service that I lose myself. I
also found that my action, even though it is in the service
of others, stops being very compassionate or even, at a
certain point, effective. I get tired, impatient, and frustrated when my actions don't bear fruit or people don't
respond or I can't accomplish my goals. How can one
balance the need to work on oneself, to pay attention to
what is going on inside, with the need to be of service to
others, without getting lost in either pursuit?

Dalai Lama: In the beginning of Buddhist practice, our ability to serve others is limited. The emphasis is on healing ourselves, transforming our mind and heart. But as we continue, we become stronger and increasingly able to serve others. But until that time, we may get overwhelmed by the suffering and difficulties of other people. We may become exhausted and not able to serve others effectively, not to mention ourselves. So we must begin simply by doing as well as we can, trying to improve ourselves, and, at the same time, trying as much as we can to serve other people. It is natural to feel some limitation with both, and we just have to accept that.

Jack Engler: Thank you, that is very helpful to hear. At first I thought you were saying that we need to do a certain amount of work in improving and healing ourselves before we can act in the world, but I think we can't wait until we've reached some ideal of development before we act. We have to act all of the time. I think that spiritual practice often encourages the belief that we have to develop ourselves first, then we'll be able to act without hurting anyone because we'll know exactly what to do. It is good to hear what you just said because I think that corrects that misinterpretation.

Dalai Lama: There are different approaches. We may engage in meditation, even over many years, with the simple motivation of wanting to improve ourselves. "I want to attain liberation. I want to overcome the afflictions of my mind."

In the context of bodhisattva practice, however, the emphasis is to be of service to others. In the course of that, as we are very actively engaged in serving others, if our own personal practice diminishes a little, we can say, "It was worthwhile because I was of some service."

Jean Shinoda Bolen: Your Holiness, we often view a person who will tolerate suffering as a candidate for sainthood. It seems to me that if you cannot help make a difference, it is important that you not be poisoned by what is being done to you; that is, that you maintain compassion, or you maintain the kind of attitude in the awful story of the saint who allowed his arm to be cut off and his leg to be cut off and all of that. If you cannot stop what is being done, then not to be poisoned or turned into a negative person yourself is all you can do.

Here in the United States, there has been an emphasis since early in our history on freedom from oppression. I feel there is a very strong need at times to stand up for what we believe is right. To act in a compassionate way may be to say, "You cannot treat me that way. If I let you abuse me, not only does it make me feel bad, but it is bad karma for you and bad for your soul. You cannot do that any more. You cannot hit me. You cannot dominate me." In our culture, most of us have an opportunity to say, "I won't allow this," and that taking a stand in this way should be encouraged, because doing nothing is a choice that has consequences. Two sayings come to mind that remind us that this is so: "Silence is consent," and, "All it takes for evil to triumph is for good people to do nothing." I think it goes beyond the personal sphere; often it is necessary to intervene, to act on behalf of someone else as well. If I am seeing something happen in front of me that I could change and I just watch it compassionately, it is not enough. If I can stop an adult from violating a child, then it is my responsibility to act compassionately and do so.

I am speaking much more for an activist compassion than we often do as psychotherapists, or as spiritual practitioners. I am really appreciative, Your Holiness, for the spirit in which I feel affirmed by the comments you have made. I would really appreciate it if you would comment more on this activist position: Is it enough simply to be compassionate, or must we act with compassion?

Dalai Lama: It is not enough to be compassionate. You must act. There are two aspects to action. One is to overcome the distortions and afflictions of your own mind, that is, in terms of calming and eventually dispelling anger and so forth. This is action out of compassion. The other is more social, more public. When there is something that needs to be done in the world to rectify the wrongs with a motivation of compassion, if one is really concerned with benefiting others, it is not enough simply to be compassionate. There is no direct benefit in that. With compassion, one needs to be engaged, involved.

Daniel Goleman: Your Holiness, what is it that allows some people to be so much more open to serving than others?

Dalai Lama: Some people do not see the opportunity or do not have the ability to serve. From a Buddhist perspective, it is that very limitation that is an incentive for spiritual practice. It varies from individual to individual whether to serve. There are various propensities and inclinations, and there is also short-term effectiveness and long-term effectiveness. The situation is complex.

It really comes down to motivation. If you can proceed in service with the purest of motivation, then no matter what comes, you can proceed sincerely and without any regret. In my own case, there is no clear criterion. Whether I am meeting with a large group of people or a few individuals, in each case I try with sincerity and pure motivation to be of the greatest service I can. How effective it is, in the short term or in the long term, there is no way to tell. All I can do is engage with complete sincerity. Then, whatever happens, there is no regret.

Sometimes you see those who, despite very sincere motivation, hesitate too much. That is an obstacle. While you are idling in hesitation, trying over and over to decide what to do, the opportunity may be lost.

Daniel Goleman: There is also the problem of preoccupation. A psychological experiment was conducted with students at a well-known divinity school who were given the parable of the Good Samaritan to study. This is a story from the Bible. A man along the side of the road is hurt, and three people pass by and do not help him. Then one man stops and helps, and he is called the Good Samaritan.

The divinity students were walking together to another building to give a talk about this story, and on the way over, they passed someone in a doorway who was moaning, "Oh, help me, help me." None of them stopped. They were all thinking about this noble idea that they were going to talk about—how to help people.

Dalai Lama: They were simply lacking in mindfulness, caught up in what they were talking about and missing the opportunity to do it.

Daniel Goleman: But you see, Your Holiness, we are all occupied most of the time with our petty concerns.

Dalai Lama: Yes, yes.

Daniel Goleman: And we pass so many opportunities to stop and help.

Daniel Brown: In Western social psychology research on altruistic action it has been discovered that many people, in situations where they could be of help to people, do not help. They simply ignore the situation. In fact, only a small number of people respond and help. Researchers have tried to understand what are the reasons, what motivates helpfulness. They have found that often, it is not empathy, love, or kindness, but outrage. The person sees something wrong and on some level says, "This is wrong. This is absolutely, unequivocally wrong. I must help." Likewise, there have been studies on sexual victimization of children. The typical response on the part of survivors is usually outrage. And as they grow up, if they get healed from this, one of the outcomes often is to use this outrage as a kind of positive motivation to help others so they don't get victimized or traumatized. This outrage can be, at times, we find, a very positive motivation because it can lead to compassionate action.

Dalai Lama: In Buddhism, we see that the motivation at the start of an action and the motivation during the action may be different. For example, you may start out with compassion, but, once you are immersed in action, anger, outrage, and hostility may enter in. The practice is not to let these overwhelm your motivation. If your heart is filled with compassion, if you've experienced what is called the "perfection of compassion," then your action is going to be pure all the way through. But until you reach that state, it may be that you start out with compassion and then become filled with outrage and other emotions.

Daniel Goleman: We find the opposite, that this is starting with outrage.

Dalai Lama: But even if you do not call it compassion, isn't there a real concern for the rights of other people and an outrage that their rights are not being met? The cherishing of the rights of other people is very close to compassion.

Daniel Brown: It is clear to us that the initial motivation of outrage is stronger and more energized than that of love. But why do some people respond with outrage and say, "This is absolutely wrong. I must help," while other people do not?

Dalai Lama: Compassion, in the Buddhist context, is the desire to relieve others of suffering. Loving kindness, or love, is the desire to bring others to happiness. That does seem to be present.

Daniel Brown: So it may be that the people who have the strong responsive outrage are the people who initially have that compassion?

Dalai Lama: For example, if someone is abused or violated in some way and experiences much suffering from that, when on a later occasion he witnesses someone else undergoing a similar abuse and wishes this other person be free from what he has experienced himself, this would be called compassion.

Daniel Goleman: Please allow me to give another example. Alcoholism is a big problem in this culture. Many people are addicted to alcohol, and usually in families where this goes on, no one speaks out. Although it is causing great pain for the person who is alcoholic and for everyone else in the family, there is silence. People may be frightened to say something. How can someone who is living in the presence of pain and caught in this web, feeling frightened of saying anything, find the courage to take the compassionate act, which is to say, "This is terrible," to express anger, to speak up. This is a very big problem.

Dalai Lama: With the case of an alcoholic, if someone in the family feels, "If I were to say something, it could very well be beneficial," and then he or she doesn't do it, this is wrong. But if one really feels, "It is not going to do any good anyway. The person is not going to listen, and my speaking out may make it even worse," then there may be reasons for not standing up and making a point.

Daniel Goleman: When people do not speak out, usually it is because of fear. Fear, for instance, that if you speak out, the person will get very angry, that the family might dissolve.

Dalai Lama: That is also a point. It can happen. So for example, if you are confronting this person about the alcoholism, even if what you are saying is correct, if your approach is not skillful, if you are too harsh, too abusive— the person is already suffering because of the alcoholism— you may simply add more suffering on top of that. Things are relative. There are no absolutes. Usually we must speak the truth. But in some cases, if we speak the truth, the consequences may be disastrous. Because of that, where the truth itself would injure and not be at all of benefit, it may be better for the time being to remain silent.

For example, imagine a monk being asked by one hundred people who are pursuing an animal if he has seen it. If the monk has seen the animal go by, what should he do? As a monk, generally speaking, he has to tell the truth. But in this situation, if he speaks truthfully, the hundred people will find the animal and kill it. So, under such circumstances, it is better not to tell the truth.

Daniel Goleman: What if, for example, you work for a corporation that is cheating people or manufacturing nuclear weapons?

Dalai Lama: If you see a wrong, if your hesitation to speak out is because of your own self-cherishing—you feel, "Oh, what will happen to me? Maybe people won't like me," and with that attitude you don't speak out, that is wrong. But if you are really chiefly concerned with others and you feel that in this particular case it would not be beneficial to speak out, then not speaking out may be appropriate.

Daniel Goleman: What about a situation where there is some social wrong, some injustice in society? You are not directly involved in it, but you see it. Is it your duty, out of compassion, to speak out? Many of us don't bother. There are so many things that we could be speaking out about, but it does not seem to have much to do with our daily lives, so we just ignore it.

Dalai Lama: That is a lack of responsibility. It is completely wrong. We must change that kind of attitude. That is why I always talk about the sense of universal responsibility. Even if someone else says, "This is our own business," or "This is an internal affair," we must speak out anyway.

Daniel Goleman: If it is your own government?

Dalai Lama: Of course you speak out. Especially in this democratic country, that is the principle; isn't it? Speak out.

Daniel Goleman: I agree.

Dalai Lama: I have heard a number of accounts in this country of murders within families, sometimes spouses, sometimes a parent or child, simply shooting—the parents shooting children and vice versa. What is your explanation of this? What are the real causes? First of all, I want to know, is this something in reality? Or is it because of the media that we see these negative things so frequently? Is it just because you publicize these things more, or is the actual rate higher?

Daniel Goleman: I believe the actual rate of such incidences is higher in America than elsewhere in the world. There are guns in many families here. It makes it very easy for a fight to escalate into a killing. Sometimes half the calls that police make in certain cities are to settle family fights that sometimes become murder. The question is why.

Dalai Lama: Is it simply because they have the weapons?

Stephen Levine: There seems to be more child abuse here also. I have talked to many people who have done this work over a long period of time and have heard a lot of intimate stories. Elisabeth Kübler-Ross, for example, says that sexual abuse and violence in this country is definitely increasing.

As you were saying before, if we have one friend, it is a miracle in life. If someone loves us, we may be able to touch the love inside ourselves. But as families have broken up in this country, we have moved farther away from the heart space the child felt secure in. I think there is enormous loneliness, and we just hate it. We feel so separate from ourselves, so separate from anything that is love. When people feel so unloved, they see everyone as an object. They even look at themselves as some foreign "thing," as something "other," of little value. I think that they have lost any sense of their own great nature. They have even lost trust that there is such a thing. They don't believe it. They feel that there is no liberation.

Dalai Lama: How do you explain this?

Stephen Levine: We feel so separate, so unable to touch the pain in ourselves, that we cause pain to others, we injure others. There seems to be more violence, hatred, and fear in the world than ever before, and so it is easier to do violence. There is more permission and less reason not to. There is less inside of us that would stop the violence. The heart does not meet the mind's confusion. There is an imbalance.

Dalai Lama: What is the source of child abuse? Why is it increasing?

Daniel Brown: The answer is complex. There are many factors, some well understood and some not. One factor is the breakdown of family and community. Because people feel more isolated, they tend to treat others in a less personal, less humanized way.

A second factor is what we call "social modeling"—we see many examples of violence. For example, in studies in which children watched adults punch an inflated plastic doll, over and over, afterwards, the children would punch others during spontaneous play. Adults served as models for this kind of behavior. Many people feel that the emphasis on violence on television and in the movies provides some of the basis for this social modeling.

A third factor is the availability of weapons and other means of violence.

A fourth factor has something to do with the state of consciousness. In domestic violence, when people fight and get to the point of hurting or murdering a spouse or a child, it is because they are in an altered state of consciousness, a different state of consciousness. Sometimes that state of consciousness can be induced by alcohol or drugs, such as cocaine. Sometimes the level of emotional intensity induces the state. A person can get into such an intense state of anger that he simply does not perceive his spouse as a person. His anger takes over. In such a state, one can do things that, later, in a normal state of consciousness, he may not even remember, or if he does remember, he remembers with or without guilt. But in that state, one does not have control over oneself. Some people have described that state as one of intense panic and rage, where they feel out of control, and there is no awareness of self and other. Others have described that state as evocative of images of a powerful, dominating self exerting force over a weak, submissive other. When these feelings and states arise within intimate relations, there is an even greater intensity and energy.

Daniel Goleman: One additional important factor is social and economic. Over the last twenty years, the wealthy people in this country have gotten much richer, while the poor people have gotten much poorer. There are many more families that have a single, unmarried mother with several children and no income except for what the government will give them, which is not enough. Many people in the United States live on the edge of desperation. They are easily pushed over the edge because their life is so hard.

Jean Shinoda Bolen: What we really are seeing is violent men behaving violently towards women and children. Of course women are involved from time to time, but mostly the question is, "Why are men doing this?"

Studies have shown that it has to do with a lack of bonding, or compassion, with their own children or with their wives. How is it that they can beat up or sexually violate their own child or their own wife? How can they do that?

In our culture it seems that men are lonelier, angrier, and more isolated than women. There is something about the way we raise boys into men that is very sad.

The feeling of love and compassion does not grow in so many American families because of what occurred in the previous generation. What was done to you, you turn around and do to the next generation. The man who does violence to his children was probably a victim of violence himself. And so how can we change that, how can we bring about feelings of love rather than anger?

There does seem to be some evidence of change, however. Fathers are often present in the delivery rooms when their babies are born. Some father instincts are motivated, and compassion for the child is born. If you have bonded with your child, you wouldn't dream of abusing him or her at age three or four or six.

Dalai Lama: Do you think that there are any hereditary influences here, purely physical? It is certainly clear that health conditions do influence the body, which influences the whole personality. But do you think that there may be hereditary influences here, transmission through the genes, from parent to child?

Daniel Goleman: Your Holiness, I think the evidence is that it is more a social influence than a biological one that causes this.

Jean noted that many adults who were beaten as children grow into parents who beat their own children. An important question is: Why do some of these abused children become parents who beat their children and some not? The strongest influence that has been found to make a difference has been if the child who is being beaten felt loved by one person in his life, maybe a relative, or even a neighbor. Those are the children who do not go on to repeat the violence.

Jean Shinoda Bolen: I do not entirely agree with Dan. I have been very impressed by people I've worked with who were badly abused, and I have wondered why they weren't, in turn, abusers. More of them were women than men. It seems that women, or girls, do not identify as much with the parent who beat them. It also seems that some people are "old souls" who are more in touch with an archetype or a pattern of meaning in themselves. And so, even as children being abused, they have a notion that they do not deserve it.

Dalai Lama: Please do not misunderstand the concept of karma. There seems to be a tendency in the West to say, "It's my karma," and then feel apathetic or fatalistic. This is not the point. We can say, "This is karma," but whose karma? If it is something you are experiencing, then it is something you yourself have brought about.

Who creates your karma? It is you who creates your own karma. But once you have engaged in an unwholesome act, there is always something you can do about it. Understanding karma does not lead to a sense of apathy, but to even greater vigor.

Jean Shinoda Bolen: In that way, a psychotherapist can be said to be someone who helps a person deal with his or her bad karma.

Dalai Lama: That is quite true.

Daniel Brown: Recently, attempts have been made to introduce moderating influences in the case of violence and abuse in the home. For example, if a professional or anyone in the community suspects that there might be child abuse or sexual abuse in some home, it is the law that they must report this to a child protection agency, which then has to investigate to find out whether or not the complaint is true. This system is still imperfect. Sometimes when the child protection agency goes into the home and discloses the secret of the abuse, it has a disruptive influence on the entire family, not just the perpetrator, and the family then blames the child, who feels traumatized again. And sometimes when the district attorney's office does investigate and presses charges, the offender may be put on trial and even go to jail. That also causes a disruption in the family, and sometimes threatens the financial stability and the whole structure of the family.

Nevertheless, there is a value in such a practice in that it forces this very isolated, abusive family to be in contact with the rest of society. It forces them to become part of the rest of the community and to pay attention to some of the social rules and norms.

Dalai Lama: The whole discussion here in the West seems to be very action-oriented. When there is abuse, you counter the abuse. When there is a violation, you counter the violation. But is there much investigation about the causes and really trying to get to the source? For example, in Buddhist practice, the first noble truth is that suffering exists. But we don't simply say, "We don't like suffering." We look for the source of suffering. That is where our real energy goes. Is there something comparable here in the West?

Daniel Brown: It is complex. There are many levels of causes, and in each individual situation, some of those causes may be more important than others.

Dalai Lama: Let's look at the situation of the media. In television and so forth, there is a very strong daily emphasis on sex and violence. I doubt that the people who are producing this really want to injure society. They simply want financial gain. That is where their priority lies. They seem to have little sense of social responsibility. On the other hand, the public seems to like the sensations from seeing these kinds of programs on television. So the public is also responsible. What can be done about this, where both of these influences are present?

Daniel Goleman: Your Holiness, I think it is very important that you point out that the public has a very large appetite for sex and violence and that the people who are producing these shows cater to this appetite. They are giving people what they want. Because so many people seem to want this, the demand is there. And because people are motivated by money, they do it. Whether they should police themselves better, whether they need more responsibility, you know, as an industry, I think that is one point.

Dalai Lama: Or at least restrain themselves.

Daniel Goleman: Or restrain themselves, yes. Maybe they don't have to be so violent or so sexual in what they depict.

The First Amendment to the American Constitution protects freedom of expression. In our society, the problem is balancing letting people be free to say what they want to say and show what they want to show and see what they want to see, and the social and psychological effects. We do not have a good answer yet. Perhaps you can suggest something.

Dalai Lama: I don't know. That is why I am asking you. It is very useful to get new ideas, new knowledge. That is very good. So as we discuss this and keep it in our thoughts, even sleep on these thoughts, then in future opportunities when we have other meetings like this, we can come up with new ideas. As I mentioned, every individual has a responsibility to try to reduce these kinds of negative things.

Jean Shinoda Bolen: For example, we might try to do a media campaign about the benefits of compassion for reducing violence in the home or for reducing one's blood pressure for better health.

Dalai Lama: Yes, yes. I always make this point. When you are mentally happy, you also become more healthy physically, and everyone wants to be more healthy physically. So it is for your benefit to be happier mentally. Happiness is one of the best methods to have a healthy body. I completely agree. What you are saying is true.

Jean Shinoda Bolen: It is important that we see examples of that. You have been asked, "How is it you maintain your joyfulness in the face of everything that is happening in Tibet?" And that you do maintain it is an important example for us.

Audience Question: I understand that among the Tibetan people, there is a lot less incidence of family violence. What do the families in Tibet do differently so that there is that much less violence?

Dalai Lama: It is not to say that there was never any violence in the homes in Tibet. But when it happened, people tended to be amazed. It was rather rare. The same was true of divorce in Tibet. It would happen, on occasion, but when it did, people would raise their eyebrows in surprise. That signified that it was an unusual event.

In traditional Asia, in terms of relationships within the family, it was probably a better situation than exists today in the West. There was a very strong emphasis on the extended family, on family ties and family harmony. With the onslaught of Western influence, this cherishing of the extended family in Asia has gradually diminished, and it is more common today to see people living in nuclear families. Traditional Asians feel that a lot has been lost in this process. In fairness, I must add that one time I met an Indian gentleman who explained to me that in his family, there were two hundred people. I think this is too much.

Audience Question: Your Holiness, do we have an obligation to stand up to someone who is harming us, or should we just offer them our forgiveness and compassion?

Dalai Lama: Tolerance and patience should not be read as signs of weakness. They are signs of strength. But tolerance and patience do not mean you accept whatever consequences develop. Tolerance means that you should not develop anger or hatred. But in an actual situation, if another person does something harmful to us, and if we still remain humble, the person may take even more advantage of us and even more negative action may come.

So, we must analyze the situation. If the situation requires some counter-measure, we can take it effectively, without anger. In fact, we will see that the action is even more effective if it is not motivated by anger. Without anger, if we analyze the situation slowly and carefully, and then take action, we are much more likely to hit the target directly!

Audience Question: Could you address the situation where a person harms another, not intentionally but because of his or her own limitations? Is this person an enemy? What do you do with the feeling of hurt?

Dalai Lama: First of all, you should recognize that person is not an enemy. If the other person has injured you unintentionally and you still feel the sense of hurt, the point here is to go back and refresh your own memory that it was unintentional. If you still have some resentments, recognize that this is a deluded response. It can happen that sometimes another person will engage in an action with a general type of attitude that could be injurious, but without specifically identifying you as a target. And so, as this person is carrying through with the action, you may be injured as a bystander. In that respect, one would say that the person does have an intention to harm.

Once again, going right back to the question, where the person harms you out of his own limitations, you simply have to say, it is not this person's fault, he simply wasn't able to do any better. Some people get so angry at themselves that they beat themselves on the head! There's not much reason to get angry. It's not a very reasonable state of mind. It can be a real headache!

Audience Question: Your Holiness, how can we act compassionately in relation to an opponent or an enemy?

Dalai Lama: By taking a wider perspective. You see that that individual is also a living creature, and you have the awareness that all living creatures are the same in wanting to be happy and avoid suffering. That realization can help you develop compassion.

If you already have compassion, you only need to include that person in the group of beings you already have compassion for. But if you don't already have compassion for all beings, it is more difficult to cultivate compassion for someone who has arisen as your enemy.

So if you do not have compassion for all sentient beings and you are simply focusing on this one person who is your enemy, wanting to feel compassion for him, it is very difficult. You may be able to say, "Compassion," but you will not be able to do much more than that.

Margaret Brenman-Gibson: Your Holiness, earlier you said that one must educate oneself about "What is the context in which I live? Where can I make a difference? How can I make a difference?—whether it is in my family, in the larger society, or the planet." This question involves mindfulness to the *nth* degree, in all areas of life, does it not? You asked us to bring examples, large or small, of compassionate actions that have made a difference. I should like to offer an example of a nonviolent action by one person who, in a liberating transformation of his own consciousness, performed a piece of civil disobedience that may be, in its specifics, singular on the stage of history. His name is Daniel Ellsberg.

As a gifted young man in his late twenties, he rose to the highest levels of the U.S. government, and he had access to many secrets of government. In the early 1960s, President Kennedy asked him to write the plans for nuclear war. Feeling himself in a position to help prevent nuclear war by making "good plans," he agreed to do it. In fact, since he first heard about the atom bomb, his life mission had been to prevent nuclear war. But finally, he came to the place where he asked himself, "How many lives are we risking here if something goes wrong and we don't prevent nuclear war?" So he asked the Joint Chiefs of Staff, "Have you figured out how many people will be dead within the first few months if something goes wrong and we don't prevent nuclear war?"

Very calmly, they said, "It will be, in the first few months, 625 million people."

He was very disturbed that they could say such a figure so calmly. So he wondered, "Who are these men I'm working with? I drink beer with them. They are very nice to their wives, their children, even their dogs. And then they announce this kind of preparation for an all out, general nuclear war." So horrified was he by this that he asked himself, "How can I reveal this to the American public?" It was a source of great anguish for him.

Then came the Vietnam War. In the beginning it was his feeling that we were going to Vietnam to liberate these people. But as it became clear that nothing of the sort was happening, he decided to go to Vietnam and see for himself what was happening.

So he went, and he became aware that it was a disaster, a most sinful endeavor. And he said, "The Vietnamese people became as familiar to me as my own hands." He meant, "We are all interdependent, part of the entire planet and all humanity." When he became clear that the war must be ended, he began to think, "How can I make this clear to the American public?"

When he came back to the U.S., he attended the lecture of a young man from Harvard, named Randy Keeler, who said, "I am on my way to prison. I have to go to prison rather than go and kill my brothers."

Hearing this, Dan Ellsberg had a transformation of consciousness, which he later described this way: "At that moment, my life split in two. I went to the men's room, sat on the floor, and cried for an hour."

At the end of that hour, he asked himself, "What can I do in my position in government to tell the American people the truth of what is going on?" And he decided to reveal to the American people how they were being lied to and how the people of Vietnam were being destroyed. "I will go to prison forever for what I'm about to do," and he revealed what are now known as the "Pentagon Papers," the secret files from the Pentagon, to *The New York Times.* When he went on trial, it turned out he did not go to prison.

I am telling this story to show how someone, in the context of his particular life, found a way to make a difference. His revealing the truth to the American people at that time of the situation in Vietnam resulted in helping end the war. The question I would like to ask Your Holiness is: How can each of us, in the context of our own lives, find the place where we have the leverage or the power to make a real difference through compassionate action? How can each of us be agents and helpers for change to foster compassion when we live in a culture where the public consciousness is dominated by war, violence, conflict, and material consumption?

Dalai Lama: From one perspective, in a situation of crisis, as our contemporary situation is, it is most important to reflect on the disadvantages of hatred and hostility, and contemplate the benefits of living a more compassionate way of life. So, on the one hand, it is true that this is a period of crisis, when there is a lot of violence and aggression. But on the other hand, we can see many hopeful signs. We hear even major politicians, such as someone in the Labor Party in Great Britain, emphasizing the importance of compassion. There may be an increasing awareness of the importance of compassion. For example, if we organized a seminar like this one in the 1950s or early '60s, only a few people would have attended. Today we are nearly one thousand. This is also a hopeful sign. We can see for ourselves the practical benefits of compassion, in terms of bringing about more contentment, serenity, and well-being. This increase in society's awareness of the importance of compassion stems from the recognition that compassion is very beneficial in one's life. It is very important to try to spread this awareness through media and education.

I have another question. Human beings are generally more intelligent than other mammals, but we also have a lot more problems that seem to correspond with our heightened intelligence. Do you think the more intelligent animals tend to have more problems than the less intelligent?

Daniel Brown: From what little I know about studies on dolphins and whales, they seem to be more protective of their community of similar animals and their species than humans are. Humans have a very large cortex on the top of the older mammalian brain. It means we have more thoughts. The suggestion may be that we need to quiet our thoughts so that we don't cause so much trouble to ourselves and others.

Daniel Goleman: When the cortex is being run by desire or anger, humans can do a lot of damage.

Dalai Lama: Another thing I have noticed is that certain ants, for example, have to work together for their survival. They have a very good sense of responsibility. They have no religion, no compassion, and no education, but somehow they have a very good sense of responsibility. We human beings are basically social animals. We have to live together. Without others, we cannot survive. Yet, we always fight. We find it very difficult to develop that kind of sense of responsibility. Why is that?

Margaret Brenman-Gibson: The range of options for human beings is much wider. We have more choices. Although there are fighting ants, generally speaking in ant colonies where survival depends on cooperative teamwork, usually the programming within the ant is much more narrow. There aren't so many choices. Human beings, with their large cortex, are different.

Dalai Lama: So intelligence is a big difference.

Margaret Brenman-Gibson: Yes, exactly.

Jack Engler: I think there is also another reason. With this large cortex, human beings have the capacity to imagine a future and imagine getting what we don't have. We also have the capacity to remember the past in a way that brings with it certain advantages, but also the capacity to be enormously frustrated when we don't get what we want. To know what other people have that we do not have can also be frustrating. That is part of the risk that comes along with this increased capacity.

Margaret Brenman-Gibson: Greed, competitiveness, and war, really.

Audience Question: Sometimes, I find it extremely difficult to live in a society so full of hatred. I often think of the solitude of death. I would like to hear your thoughts on this, Your Holiness.

Dalai Lama: We really don't have a hundred percent guarantee, do we, that when we die, we're going to find the peace and the happiness that we long for. As long as we are alive as human beings, there is something that we can do about it. So, I think that is the major thing to do, to live as a human being. It is a great mistake simply to regard this whole life, this whole existence as fruitless and pointless and to think about suicide.

You see, we have such a beautiful human brain and a beautiful human heart. By combining these two things, I think we can solve every problem. I believe, we need only a little more patience and determination. So don't worry. There is no point in engaging in foolish anxiety.

Audience Question: In our Western society, Your Holiness, external achievements, such as how much money people make or what position they have, whether they're presidents of companies, are indicators of success. What are measures of success in Tibetan society?

Dalai Lama: In terms of secular life in Tibet, the notion of success is more or less the same as here. But for those who are more drawn to the spiritual dimension, inner realization, the quality of awareness, is what constitutes success.

Jean Shinoda Bolen: Your Holiness, in many parts of the world women are treated as lesser beings over whom men have power, and this creates many kinds of oppression, ranging from lack of education, to inferior working conditions, to sexual and physical abuse. What is a Tibetan Buddhist's attitude towards women? Are men considered spiritually superior to women in Tibetan Buddhism, and what are the essential differences between the sexes? I also want to ask one question: Does Your Holiness recall any previous lives as a woman?

Dalai Lama: Not only can I not recall my experiences in my previous lives, sometimes I can't even remember what I did yesterday. As a Buddhist, you know, I accept and believe in the theory of rebirth. So there is no question that in my previous lives, there were definitely many lives as women. And in future lives also, it is not certain whether I will be reborn with a female body or a male body or some other form of body. I don't know. The most important thing in Buddhism is no discrimination. The ultimate aim is the same for men and women. In the capacity to achieve nirvana, or Buddhahood, there are no differences.

But in the *Vinaya,* the rules concerning monastic discipline, it says that any fully-ordained male monk is placed in a position of seniority over any ordained nun. According to the *Sutrayana,* as well as the teachings in the lower tantras, in the very moment one attains the full awakening of Buddhahood, it is said to be necessary to be male. But, ultimately, according to the same teachings, there are no differences. So from the perspective of the highest dimension of Buddhist practice, *The Highest Yoga Tantra*, there is no distinction. Even in that final life in which you attain Buddhahood, there is no difference whether you are male or female. In this system, there are more concerns about females than about males. For example, there are a number of root downfalls in the context of this *Highest Yoga Tantra* practice. One of these root downfalls is for a male to abuse or to look down upon a female. If a man does that, it is disastrous. There is no comparable downfall for a woman looking down on a man. So we men are jealous.

In Tibetan society, which is a different issue, there is not much difference in status or position of males and females. In Tibet, we did not even know about that kind of discrimination until later when we saw it in India and China.

Jean Shinoda Bolen: Can you ever imagine being reincarnated as a woman Dalai Lama?

Dalai Lama: Of course, that's possible. There are many female reincarnated lamas, spiritual leaders. One is a very famous lama, considered very high. In terms of lamas, or spiritual teachers in the Tibetan tradition, there is not much distinction between men and women. The point is whether your practice is good, whether you have gained high realization. If you have, then you are bound to have students and become a lama.

There is a true feminist movement in Buddhism that relates to the goddess Tara. Following her cultivation of *bodhicitta*, the bodhisattva's motivation, she looked upon the situation of those striving towards full awakening and she felt that there were too few people who attained Buddhahood as women. So she vowed, "I have developed bodhicitta as a woman. For all of my lifetimes along the path I vow to be born as a woman, and in my final lifetime when I attain Buddhahood, then, too, I will be a woman." This is true feminism.

Audience Question: What can we do to help reduce the suffering of the Earth? How can we strengthen our love for and our service to the living Earth?

Dalai Lama: This planet is our own home. Taking care of our world, our planet, is just like taking care of our own house. We need to take care of our house. Our very lives depend upon this Earth, our environment.

The Earth is, to a certain extent, our mother. She is so kind, because whatever we like to do, she tolerates it. But now, the time has come when our power to destroy is so extreme that Mother Earth is compelled to tell us to be careful. The population explosion and many other indicators make that clear, don't they? Nature has its own natural limitations.

Another way to approach this question is to see that in the same way that this body is composed of different elements, so the planet itself is also composed of different elements. There are simply natural laws. If we try to break them, we will not meet with success, no matter how sophisticated we become or how many complex missions we undertake.

Audience Question: Will humanity be able to preserve the planet's beauty before it is destroyed?

Dalai Lama: I think so. I'm always optimistic. I think it is not too late. In the early, or even the middle part of this century, very few people were concerned about the natural environment. Today, there are even political parties whose ideologies are based on ecology. That is a very positive development, so, I am very hopeful.

Daniel Goleman: Your Holiness, with modern technology, the way we live our daily lives, the things we use every day, the things we buy, the things we throw away—when you multiply them by four billion, very minor acts have vast consequences for the planet. Is there a role for something like mindfulness in this compassion for the planet, where we can be more attentive to the things we buy heedlessly. How can each of us be more heedful, more mindful of what we're doing to our mother?

Dalai Lama: It is awareness itself, mindfulness. Simply be more aware. Education is very important, and also a sense of responsibility. First of all, we need education, so that we know what we are to be mindful of. We have to have that first in order to open our eyes. Then when we are engaged in life, we encounter situations that correspond to what we have learned about in theory in our education. What mindfulness is concerned with, then, is really focusing in on those actual situations, being aware of them and responding appropriately. Mindfulness goes hand in hand with education. From this will certainly come a cherishing of the environment. The potential, the possibility, is always there for everyone. Even a simple act, such as throwing away the trash, although it might seem insignificant, when we multiply it by billions of others who might do the same thing, can have an enormous impact.

Thinking in such terms, everyone can find the context where they can make a difference. The human community, humanity, is nothing but individuals combined. This morning, a television interviewer asked me whether I consider myself a peacemaker, and I told her, "No, I am just a human being." Peace is something for everyone, and each individual human being is responsible for it. From that viewpoint, each person is a peacemaker. I am just trying to do my share.

If you want to change the world, first try to improve, change, within yourself. That will help change your family. From there it just gets bigger and bigger. Everything we do has some effect, some impact. This is my basic belief. Wherever I go, I am always trying to make this clear, the responsibility of the individual person. So we should never feel, "I am insignificant. What I do does not matter." Especially in America, a democratic country, the public's voice is very influential. I don't know anything besides that.

Jean Shinoda Bolen: Western technological societies are sorely in need of some spiritual direction at this time. Do you feel that the wisdom tradition from Tibet can help provide the kind of spiritual leadership we need at this time? Do you have a sense of fulfilling this need as a spokesperson for a tradition that the world could sorely use.

Dalai Lama: I don't know. That is difficult to say. Generally speaking, if we examine the course of history, we find that whether an individual was able to fulfill his or her mission is knowable only in retrospect, after the person has died. So, I really don't know.

Audience Question: Do you feel that Americans and the United States as a country have any special mission in the world? What do you think that Americans can contribute to world harmony and world peace?

Dalai Lama: America, like every other nation, has some good aspects and some negative aspects. That is normal. Firstly, the United States is a so-called superpower. You are a superpower, not only in military and economic force, but even more so in freedom. I think that your greatest strength is in creating a country where true, open space is available, where human individual creative nature can be fully realized. Of course, it is true that in your country there is much inequality—many people are poor while others are quite rich. But basically, there is genuine freedom here, and this is quite an open society. I think that is your real source of strength and progress.

America is a young nation—I mean the white settlers—so you still have very little culture or history. But that is good, because it helps you keep such an open attitude towards many different cultures and faiths. This nation, and particularly in this area of California, is multi-racial and multi-cultural. If you use that environment in the right way, I think it can help you to have fewer prejudices and be more receptive. Generally I find Americans to be quite straightforward and easy to understand. I like this very much.

But, sometimes I feel, in the global atmosphere of international politics, that moral uprightness or justice, has very little value, and that makes me very sad. If that continues, many people will suffer. Eventually, the superpowers will also suffer. Even though America is a powerful nation, you need genuine friends, including the small countries. How can you make friends? I think, on top of your material strength and cultural strength, you must begin to stand firm with moral principles. That would be marvelous.

The present trend is not healthy. Sooner or later you will have to change. It is easier to change while you are strong. If you become weaker or smaller, it will be much more difficult to change. You will not be strong enough to face the consequences. Powerful nations always have a greater chance and capacity to right the wrongs in our system and be able to take the risks that are involved in changing an existing system. Until the 1950s and '60s, America was a really powerful nation with quite high prestige, a real champion of liberty and freedom. But for the past thirty years, it seems to me, you have been going in the opposite direction. That is sad. But it is not my business; it is really your business.

Daniel Brown: Your Holiness, based on your knowledge of Western society, what emphasis would you recommend for us—working on ourselves or serving others?

Dalai Lama: In order to serve other people, you must have strong determination and a positive motivation. From time to time, you also need to recharge yourself. So I think it is about fifty/fifty, between recharging yourself and serving other people. It depends on one's particular circumstances, but in my case, that is what I am trying to do.

Stephen Levine: Your Holiness, in order to have the kind of morality and ethics that are necessary for peace, we must have enormous courage. How can we develop that courage when there is so little support, so little reward for compassion, caring, and those kinds of efforts in this society? How do we develop the courage of Jesus to do what is right no matter what the consequences?

Dalai Lama: I don't know. If you look at this question from another point of view, you will see that the leaders of the world now have a lot of courage—the courage to do what is wrong.

Stephen Levine: Is that courage or ignorance?

Dalai Lama: It is a very complicated question. These leaders are not wise, but they are too clever, or crafty. I think these kinds of wrong policies, that is, policies that are not based on justice, are mainly due to shortsightedness. When people are shortsighted, they see short-term gains and develop the kind of courage to do what is wrong.

If any sensible person thinks deeply, he will respect justice. There is an inborn appreciation and respect for justice within our human body. In children, we find what is natural to the human character. But as they grow up, they develop a lot of conditioning and wrong attitudes. I often feel there is more truthfulness in a small child. To me this shows that in the human blood, there is some kind of respect or appreciation for the truth. I find many reasons to have confidence in human courage and human nature.

Stephen Levine: When those positive qualities do not arise, when we want to help but find ourselves afraid to, how can we call upon that natural goodness to surface, so that our fears and conditioning do not obstruct the oneness out of which this goodness arises?

Dalai Lama: I feel that education and the media can play a very important role here.

Audience Question: Your Holiness, in these darkest of times for Tibet, how do you see your mission in relation to Tibet?

Dalai Lama: I don't know if I have any specific mission for the Tibetan people, but my attitude and opinion always have been to serve the Tibetan people as well as possible under the existing circumstances. The situation in Tibet is quite sad. As I mentioned, any challenge is also an opportunity. This is a crucial period of time for us to show our determination. In my own case, I am trying to do my best.

Audience Question: Do you feel you have some special mission, not only in regards to Tibet but also in relation to the whole planet, to the whole world?

Dalai Lama: Yes. I believe that every human being has this special responsibility, so naturally, I too have some responsibility.

Audience Question: Where do we go from here?

Dalai Lama: I think that getting together in groups like this, sharing our experiences, is an important way we can continue to help each other.

Margaret Brenman-Gibson: Yes, Your Holiness, we helpers often feel lonely and isolated. We can schedule large conferences like this from time to time, but I think it is even more important for like-minded peers to meet regularly in smaller groups, perhaps weekly or monthly. This is a marvelous step to help us take care of ourselves, and, accordingly, be of greater service to others.

Daniel Goleman: Your Holiness, do you have any final thoughts or questions for us to ponder as we go on our way home?

Dalai Lama: I have nothing special to offer. I myself have found these dialogues very beneficial.

AFTERWORD: GENUINE COMPASSION

H.H. the Dalai Lama

As human beings, social animals, it is quite natural for us to love. We even love animals and insects, such as the bees, who produce and collect honey. I really admire bees' sense of common responsibility. When you watch a beehive, you see that those small insects come from far away, take a few seconds' rest, go inside, and then hurriedly fly away. They are faithful to their responsibility. Although sometimes individual bees fight, basically there is a strong sense of unity and cooperation. We human beings are supposed to be much more advanced, but sometimes we lag behind even small insects.

As social animals, we human beings cannot survive alone. If we were by nature solitary, there would be no towns or cities. Because of our nature, we have to live in a cooperative setting. People who have no sense of responsibility for the society or the common good are acting against human nature. For human survival, we need genuine cooperation, based on the sense of brotherhood and sisterhood. Friends make us feel secure. Without friends, we feel a great loneliness. Sometimes, there is no proper person with whom we can communicate and share affection, so we may prefer an animal, such as a dog or a cat. This shows that even those people who lose their trusted friends need someone to communicate and share affection with. I myself like my wristwatch, even though it never shows me any affection! In order to get mental satisfaction, as a human being, it is best to love another human being, and, if that is not possible, then some animal. If you show sincere affection, you will receive a response, and you will feel satisfaction. We all need friends.

There are different approaches to friendship. At times we may think that we need money and power to have friends, but that is not correct. When our fortune is intact, those kinds of friends may appear loyal, but when our fortune disappears, they will leave us. They are not true friends; they are friends of money or power. Alcohol is another unreliable friend. If you drink too much, you may collapse, and even your dreams will be unpleasant.

But there are other kinds of friends who, no matter what the situation, remain true. When our fortunes rise, even without friends, we can manage. But when they go down, we need true friends. In order to make genuine friends, we ourselves must create an environment that is pleasant. If we just have a lot of anger, not many people will be drawn close to us. Compassion or altruism draws friends. It is very simple.

All of the world's religions emphasize the importance of compassion, love, and forgiveness. Each may have a different interpretation, but, broadly speaking, everyone bases their understanding on the basis of brotherhood, sisterhood, and compassion. Those who believe in God usually see their love for their fellow human beings as an expression of their love for God. But if someone says, "I love God," and does not show sincere love towards his fellow human beings, I think that is not following God's teaching.

Many religions emphasize forgiveness. Love and compassion are the basis of true forgiveness. Without them, it is difficult to develop forgiveness.

Love and compassion are basic human qualities. From a Buddhist point of view, love is an attitude of wanting to help other sentient beings enjoy happiness, and compassion is the wish for other sentient beings to be free from suffering. Compassion is not a selfish attitude, such as, "These are my friends, and therefore I want them to be free of suffering." Genuine compassion can be extended even towards one's enemies, because the very basis for generating compassion is seeing suffering in other living creatures, and that includes your enemies. When you see that your enemies are suffering, you are able to develop genuine compassion even towards those who have injured you.

Usual compassion and love give rise to a very close feeling, but it is essentially attachment. With usual love, as long as the other person appears to you as beautiful or good, love remains, but as soon as he or she appears to you as less beautiful or good, your love completely changes. Even though someone appears to you as a dear friend and you love him very much, the next morning the situation may completely change. Even though he is the same person, he feels more like an enemy. Instead of feeling compassion and love, you now feel hostility. With genuine love and compassion, another person's appearance or behavior has no effect on your attitude.

Real compassion comes from seeing the other's suffering. You feel a sense of responsibility, and you want to do something for him or her. There are three types of compassion. The first is a spontaneous wish for other sentient beings to be free of suffering. You find their suffering unbearable and you wish to relieve them of it. The second is not just a wish for their well-being, but a real sense of responsibility, a commitment to relieve their suffering and remove them from their undesirable circumstances. This type of compassion is reinforced by the realization that all sentient beings are impermanent, but because they grasp at the permanence of their identity, they experience confusion and suffering. A genuine sense of compassion generates a spontaneous sense of responsibility to work for the benefit of others, encouraging us to take this responsibility upon ourselves. The third type of compassion is reinforced by the wisdom that although all sentient beings have interdependent natures and no inherent existence, they still grasp at the existence of inherent nature. Compassion accompanied by such an insight is the highest level of compassion.

In order to cultivate and develop genuine compassion within yourself, you need to identify the nature of suffering and the state of suffering that sentient beings are in. Because you want sentient beings to be free from their suffering, first of all you have to identify what suffering is. When Buddha taught the Four Noble Truths, he spoke of three types of suffering: suffering that is obvious and acute, like physical pain; the suffering of change, such as pleasurable experiences that have the potential to turn into suffering; and pervasive suffering, which is the basic fact of conditioned existence. To cultivate compassion, first of all, you have to reflect on suffering and identify suffering as suffering. When reflecting in depth on the nature of suffering, it is always beneficial to search for an alternative—to see whether it is possible to ever get rid of suffering. If there is no way out, just reflecting on suffering will make you feel depressed, and that is not helpful. If there is no possibility of getting rid of the suffering, then it is better to not think about it at all.

After describing the origin of suffering, the Buddha spoke of the cessation of suffering and the path that leads to the cessation. When you realize that it *is* possible to eliminate the root that gives rise to suffering, that awareness will increase your determination to identify and reflect on suffering at all different levels, and that will inspire you to seek liberation.

After reflecting on the nature of suffering and feeling convinced that there is a path that leads to the cessation of suffering, then it is important to see that all sentient beings do not want suffering and do want happiness. Everyone has the right to be happy, to overcome suffering. When reflecting on ourselves, we find that we have a natural desire to be happy and to overcome suffering, and that this desire is just and valid. When we see that all living creatures have the natural right to be happy and overcome suffering and fulfill their wishes, we ourselves have a spontaneous feeling of self-worth.

The only difference between us and others is in number. We are just one individual among infinite others. No matter how important we are, we are just one sentient being, one single self, while others are infinite. But there is a close relationship of interdependence. Our suffering or happiness is very much related with others. That is also reality. Under these circumstances, if, in order to save one finger the other nine fingers are sacrificed, that is foolish. But if, in order to save nine fingers, one finger is sacrificed, it may be worth it. So you see the importance of others' rights and your own rights, and others' welfare and your own welfare. Because of numbers, the infinite numbers of others' rights and welfare naturally become most important. The welfare of others is important not only because of the sheer number, but also if you were to sacrifice the infinite others for your own happiness eventually you will lose. If you think more of others, taking care of others' rights and serving others, ultimately you will gain.

Not only when you are engaging in the meditative practices of the bodhisattva path is it harmful to sacrifice the welfare and happiness of infinite others for your own happiness, as it prevents you from making progress in the spiritual path, but if you were to sacrifice the benefit and welfare of infinite others for the sake of your own happiness and welfare in your daily life, you are the one who ultimately will lose and suffer the consequences.

If you want to be selfish, you should be selfish-with-wisdom, rather than with foolishness. If you help others with sincere motivation and sincere concern, that will bring you more fortune, more friends, more smiles, and more success. If you forget about others' rights and neglect others' welfare, ultimately you will be very lonely.

Even our enemy is very useful to us because, in order to practice compassion we need to practice tolerance, forgiveness, and patience, the antidotes to anger. In order to learn tolerance, forgiveness, and patience, we need someone to create some trouble. From this point of view, there is no need to feel anger towards the enemy or the person who creates the problem for us. In fact, we should feel gratitude for the opportunity he provides us. Regardless of whether he intended to benefit us, whenever we find anything that is helpful, we can utilize the opportunity. Of course one might argue that the enemy has no conscious intention to be of help, but on the contrary, has a strong conscious intention to cause harm, and therefore, anger is justified. This is true. We categorize someone as an enemy because he has the intention to harm us. Even if a surgeon has to amputate our limb, because surgeons do not generally have the intention to harm us, we don't classify them as our enemy. Since our enemy has the intention to be harmful to us, we classify and identify him as an enemy, and therefore we have this opportunity to practice patience and tolerance toward that person.

In order to practice compassion toward all living beings, it is important to be able to generate a genuine sense of patience and tolerance toward our enemies. In order to cultivate genuine patience toward our enemy, there are certain types of mental trainings. For instance, if you have been injured by gunfire, if you feel angry, you should analyze the situation and think, what is it that I am angry at? If I am angry at the thing that injured me, I should be angry at the direct cause of my injury, which is the bullet. If I should feel anger toward the ultimate cause of my injury, I should feel anger toward the anger within the person who shot at me. But that is not the case. I don't feel angry at the bullet or the other person's anger; I feel angry at the person, who is just the medium. Under different circumstances, that person could change into a good friend.

As long as that negative emotion is there, it acts like an enemy. But when a positive motivation develops, that person becomes our friend. The person himself can be changed under different circumstances, dominated by different factors of the mind. So, logically speaking, if we are to feel anger toward the thing that harmed us, it is the *anger* within that person that we should feel angry at. So, just as we see how destructive is the anger generated within us, how it destroys our peace of mind, mental balance, and so forth, so it is in the case of the anger generated within the enemy's mind. It affects his mind and his happiness.

Therefore, when someone dominated by anger harms you, instead of feeling angry toward him, you should feel a sense of compassion and pity because that person is suffering himself. When you reflect in this way, it will help reduce the force of your anger. When you train your mind in this way, gradually you will be able to extend your compassion toward all living creatures, including your enemy.

I myself, as a Buddhist monk who is supposedly a practitioner—although my practice is very lazy and not at all satisfying to myself—even a lazy practitioner with not enough time, step by step, little by little, can change. I can change my own mental attitude, and it brings me some real joy and inner strength. Brothers and sisters, please think along these lines. If you feel you can practice at a certain point, please try to carry it out as a kind of experiment. As time goes on, you may get some benefit. But if you feel it isn't working, don't worry. Don't be concerned at all.

Compassion, or altruistic motivation, is really wonderful. Sometimes I feel a sense of wonder that we human beings can develop such altruism. It is really a precious source of inner strength, happiness, and future success.

Parallax Press publishes books and tapes on mindful awareness and social responsibility, "making peace right in the moment we are alive." It is our hope that doing so will help alleviate suffering and create a more peaceful world. Some of our recent titles include:

The First Buddhist Women, by Susan Murcott

Seeds of Peace: A Buddhist Vision for Renewing Society, by Sulak Sivaraksa

World as Lover, World as Self, by Joanna Macy

Transformation and Healing, by Thich Nhat Hanh

Dharma Gaia: A Harvest of Essays in Buddhism and Ecology, edited by Allan Hunt Badiner

In the Footsteps of Gandhi, by Catherine Ingram

The Anguish of Tibet, edited by Petra K. Kelly, Gert Bastian, and Pat Aiello

For a copy of our free catalog, please write to:

Parallax Press
P.O. Box 7355
Berkeley, California 94707